Hearts on Fire

Hearts on Fire

The Evolution
of an Urban Church

by
Bill Lane Doulos

WIPF & STOCK · Eugene, Oregon

Wipf and Stock Publishers
199 W 8th Ave, Suite 3
Eugene, OR 97401

Hearts on Fire
The Evolution of an Urban Church
By Doulos, Bill Lane
Copyright© by Doulos, Bill Lane
ISBN 13: 978-1-60899-004-7
Publication date 4/11/2016
Previously published by All Saints Church

Dedicated to George F. Regas
Rector, All Saints Church, Pasadena
1967-1995
A Celebration of a Ministry

Help us, O God, to be masters of ourselves,
that we may become the servants of others.
Take our lips and speak through them;
take our minds and think through them;
and take our hearts and set them on fire,
for Christ's sake.
Amen.

Table of Contents

Acknowledgements ix
Introduction, by George F. Regas xiii
1. Walking on God's Beaches 1
2. The Heartbeat of a New Parish 11
3. The Church as an Outpost 21
4. Gathering the Faithful 33
5. A Regimen for Renewal 41
6. Hearts on Fire 49
7. The Jury Is In 57
8. Making All Saints Famous 65
9. The Gospel Sting 73
10. The Peace Journey 81
11. Rich and Poor Together 103
12. Housing as a Cornerstone of Justice 115
13. Keepers of the Vision 125
14. The Inclusive Church 135
15. Building a Parish 145
16. Education for Ministry 157
17. A Sanctuary for Children 167
18. Just a Country Preacher 175

Acknowledgements

THE PAST SIX MONTHS have been an extraordinary feast of listening to 60 members and friends of All Saints Church in an effort to discover more about this remarkable parish in the midst of the city. I have been transformed as I have heard in detail the stories of the people who have created a great witness to the power of God let loose in the world.

Having worked with George Regas for 20 years, I am apt to take for granted many of the gifts that he brings to his ministry. Familiarity has bred in me a quiet sense of awe in response to the privilege I have shared as a member of George's staff. Some of us grow in our own faith and witness if we can find a place to root ourselves in the shadow of a giant oak. I am one such person among many on our staff and in our parish. George Regas has mediated to me the love and encouragement and challenge of the living God. And I am grateful.

I can't begin to record the names of those who have told me how much George Regas has liberated their lives. This theme emerged again and again in my research for this book.

My only regret is that I could not honor the contributions of all who told me their personal stories of renewal. Hundreds of other people, past and present members and friends, haven't even been included in my rounds of interviews. The reader probably thinks I am including every program and every person. I have chosen instead to highlight a few programs and write in more detail about a few parishioners who must be allowed for the sake of brevity to represent the lives of many others.

In the preparation of the manuscript, I am especially indebted to George Regas and his predecessor, John Burt. Anne Peterson has been my most helpful and constructive critic. I am also grateful to Peggy Phelps and Jane Olson and their committee members who have provided oversight for this work: Susan Caldwell, Jim Fullerton, Ken Rhodes and Lou Fleming. Others who have assisted in reviewing the manuscript have been Bob and Barbara Miller, Jean Fleming, John Horn, Lois Marski, Margaret Marsh, Bob and Liz Morton, and Russ Kully. Helpful ideas were provided by Frank Clark, Nelson Leonard, Jean Taylor-Lescoe and Jack Miles, and hospitality was given by Adelaide and Alexander Hixon.

In addition to many of the above, those interviewed included Edna and Ernest Banks, Adele Barnes, Leonard Beerman, Mark Benson, Jennie Bevington and Eric Seyfarth, Gary Bradley, Bill and Clara Burgess, Alice Callaghan, Lorna Carry, Nancy Casad, Marty Coleman, Dwayne Dawson, Sue Dragge, Bob Egelston, Rick and Judy Felton, Harriet Fullerton, Dick Gillett, Gary Hall, Grace Hall, Chris Hartmire, Hassan Hathout, Bob Iles, Dorothy Kilian, Dorothy Learned, Don and Lorna Miller, Sue Miner, Kristin Neily, Fran Neumann, Margaret Parker, Mary Parmenter, Ludie Paulson, Bill Rankin, Russ Reid, Betty Rhodes, Bill Rodiger, Ed Rounds and Callae Walcott-Rounds, Tim Safford, Michael Schacht, Bill and Edla Scharre, Margaret Sedenquist, John Sweetland, Lydia Wilkins, Jim Walker, and John and Denise Wood.

I am also grateful to Dave Dirckx for administrative support, and to Castle Press, and especially Fred Balian, Colleen

McKernan and Shelly Houston for their assistance.

This book has been written in commemoration of the ministry of George Regas at All Saints Episcopal Church over the past 28 years. All Saints is a forward-looking place, and we corporately believe that our best years as a parish still lie ahead. But as George retires from his position as our Rector, we must take this opportunity to pause, and to recount and honor his contribution to our lives.

BILL LANE DOULOS
Pasadena, California
October 1, 1994

George Regas and Bill Doulos leading a procession to the groundbreaking for the new Union Station site on South Raymond, September 28, 1986.

Introduction

IT WAS A LITTLE BY CHANCE and the good intuition of Ken and Betty Rhodes that I came to All Saints, Pasadena, from Nyack, New York, in May of 1967. But it was through God's grace, a lot of hard work, and the support of an incredible congregation of people, that this 36-year-old kid grew up and lived into this remarkable place. No one could have been more blessed by a congregation than I. It has been a magnificent honor to have been the Rector here for these 28 years.

Hearts on Fire is the story of this incomparable place, and describing it on paper is a Herculean task. It is impossible, in a finite number of pages, to tell the story of every person who has made a significant contribution to the history of All Saints, and to mention everyone who has had a vital part in its ongoing life. In my mind's eye I see so many faces–people who loved this church and are now in God's eternity, people who have been in my balcony encouraging me all my career, people I have just met for the first time last Sunday, following the service, at the door of the church, who were so grateful to have found a spiritual home. All these wonderful people, as well as many I don't even know, have touched All Saints and helped to give it shape and substance, vitality and vision.

I can think of no other person who could have accomplished this audacious task with such style and in such a short period of time than Bill Lane Doulos. He has been my close colleague for 20 years. During the years he was the editor of the All Saints *Bulletin*, he would meet the weekly deadline sitting at a computer terminal in the lobby of the office building, weaving a rich and witty descriptive tapestry from the threads and scraps of information given him by members of the staff. Like a great athlete going for the gold medal, he appeared to do it effortlessly.

I have always believed that the Church should be a beacon on a hill–allowing God's light to shine in a world of shadows, alerting people to the rocky shoals below the surface, and illuminating the way toward a moral and healing vision for life. But to be that beacon in such a troubled world requires risk and trust. In the activist ministry of All Saints, we've moved into deep waters and trusted God's never-failing love to be there. And not all institutions are willing to do that. I give thanks to the people of All Saints and to my staff for their willingness to venture out into the unknown places of danger and risk, led by the Spirit, in order to help bring in God's kingdom of peace and justice and healing.

I am the inheritor of a great legacy; my ministry has been built on a strong foundation. I am deeply grateful to all the rectors of this great church who have given their very best to this parish and whose prayers and leadership have sustained its people for more than a hundred years. The time has come for me to retire. I have loved the people of my parish with great intensity. In these years as Rector I have given only a part of my 64 years, but I've given the whole of my heart. I now give the care of this beloved congregation over to the next Rector, who will bring vision and energy in a new, fresh way. And the best part of all is that the incredible story of All Saints continues!

GEORGE F. REGAS
All Saints, Pasadena
November 1, 1994

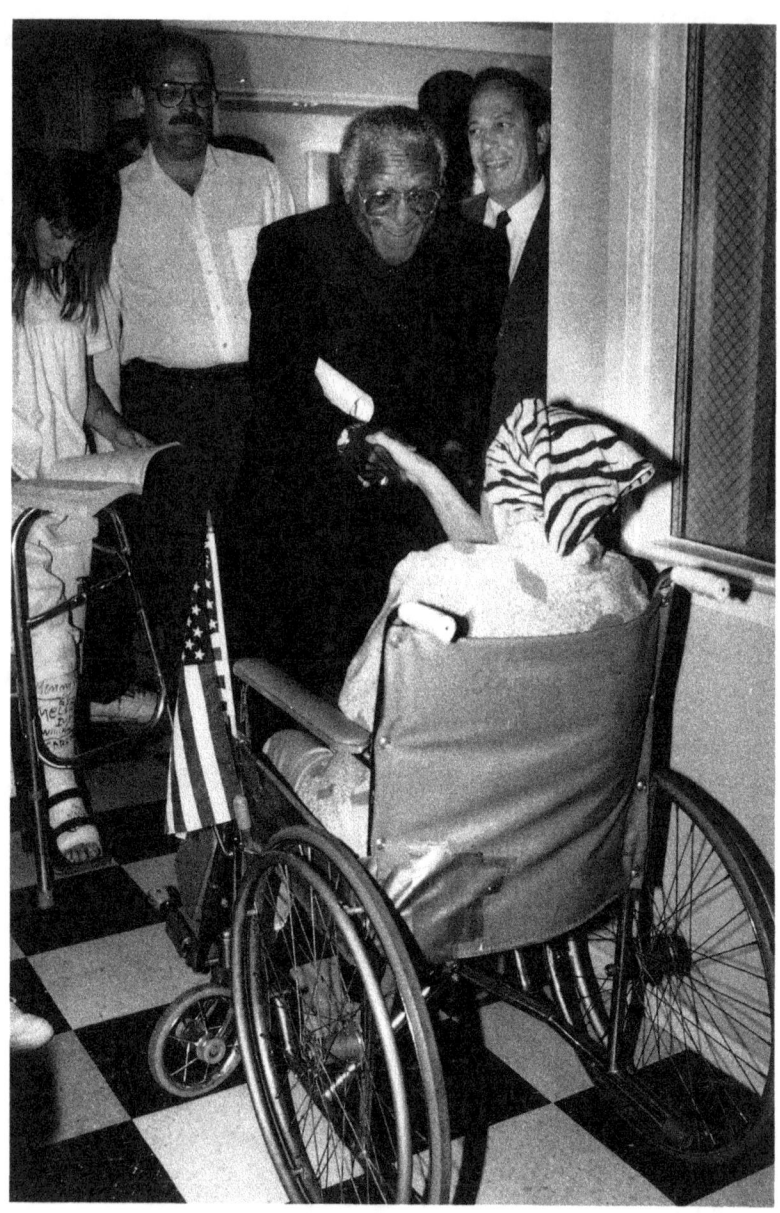

A visit from Archbishop Desmond Tutu, hosted by Bill Doulos and George Regas and the residents of Skid Row's Pershing Hotel.

Chapter 1

Walking on God's Beaches

We are seeing a veritable miracle unfold before our very eyes. We are seeing a nation come to birth. And you, friends, all of you—under George's scintillating and inspiring leadership—are a very, very substantial part of that victory. We would not be where we are without your incredible support, your love, your prayers, your caring—doing things that were unpopular, such as supporting our campaign for the imposition of sanctions. Thank you, all of you beautiful people! Thank you! Thank you! Thank you!

WITH HIS ARMS OUTSTRETCHED, Desmond Tutu stood in the pulpit of All Saints Church on June 5, 1994, before overflowing congregations at two services, to celebrate the victory in his native South Africa of the forces that had risen up against the evil of apartheid.

The bounce in his walk and the twinkle in his eyes were consistent with earlier visits to the parish, in 1982 and 1991. The spirit of celebration seemed to pervade his being, even in the depths of the struggle for his country's freedom, when he was trying to convince his fellow Anglicans on another continent that our prayers and solidarity could make a difference.

His visits were as refreshing to All Saints as they were meant to be for Desmond. He called himself a "prisoner of hope," and he called us the "beautiful people of God."

Now, in the flush of the celebration of 1994, parishioners at All Saints were hungry to taste the fruit of this triumph of faith. We had read the papers, of course. We knew that a democratic election had just been held, and that Nelson Mandela had been elected the new president of a new republic. But only our twin leaders in the struggle, Desmond Tutu, the Archbishop of Capetown, and our own Rector, George Regas, could share with us the deep spiritual meaning of this political transformation.

What kind of church was this that could engage in a political struggle in a distant land? What kind of faith would lead one to a victory half a world away?

Participation with Desmond Tutu in this epic event was authentic, not just symbolic, because this parish of All Saints had actually done some of the hard work of creating social change. The engagement of the issue of freedom for South Africa had been a consuming effort ever since George and Mary Regas had led a parish contingent of seven lay people on a South African journey in 1988. They had visited with Desmond, whom George had met a decade earlier, and many other leaders, gaining political intelligence and solidifying a friendship that would renew lives on two continents.

When our ambassadors returned to Pasadena, the parish established an international witness through a Center for South African Ministry, working under the leadership of Brian Sellers-Petersen. A strong interfaith board was formed to sponsor an educational conference and undertake lobbying and letter-writing campaigns about human rights violations and economic boycotts. A delegation went before the city councils in Los Angeles and Pasadena to enlist their support for disinvestment. The parish offered its prayers and encouragement and some financial support. Rick Felton, who chaired the board, bought a fax machine for the church so that we could keep in touch with developments. Some of the homes of parishioners were offered as places of respite for South African priests who were under intense pressure in their homeland.

As the Archbishop of Capetown, Desmond Tutu had been the leading religious advocate for this dramatic change. In speaking to his sisters and brothers in Christ at All Saints, he cited one of the turning points of his own journey.

The political powers of apartheid had once said to Desmond that black people were not allowed to walk on a particular beach. It was owned by white people, and was off limits to blacks.

Desmond was incredulous!

How could anyone claim as their exclusive possession what so obviously belonged to God? A beach is a place where the forces of nature come together in unique ways: the thunderous clapping of the ocean surf, teeming with life, crashing in upon a seemingly inert and immovable mass of endless sand. So much of who God is and who we are as the beneficiaries of God's creation is captured for us as we walk along God's beaches. So much wonder and mystery are uniquely accessible to those who are privileged to stand at the ocean's edge.

So Desmond and Nelson Mandela and thousands of their South African colleagues and millions of supporters around the globe took a stand against apartheid. The forces of God and of history, which belongs to God, were on their side. The status quo in South Africa was changed forever.

For those of us watching the events from afar the issues seemed crystal clear. Of course all God's children should be able to walk upon God's beaches. Such clarity comes normally only from geographical or chronological distance. In the turmoil of the struggle for justice, when time and place are crowding out the voice of God, when the oppressive moment gives us no perspective, truth is harder to come by.

The ability to discern eternal truth in the midst of the shadowy interplay of current events and opinions is a very rare ability. Only a few people seem to have this gift of prophetic insight. Two of them are Desmond Tutu and George Regas. And of these few who can walk into the midst of a specific place and a specific time and make a divine pronouncement, the ability to organize and mobilize people around this central truth is an even more precious gift. Truth begins at the margins of people's consciousness, and only with hard work and organization moves into the center.

One might use biblical imagery to illustrate this difference between the "pronouncement of truth" (such as when Desmond Tutu remonstrated that all of God's children ought to be able to walk on God's beaches) and the actual "arrival of truth" (such as when these children actually were able to walk on these beaches with the force of law and public opinion behind them).

The coming of Christ is heralded in scripture by the phrase, "the voice of one crying in the wilderness." Here is the divine insight by the lone prophet, John the Baptist in this case, proclaiming the arrival of truth. But nothing seems to change on the basis of this verbal assault, and unless you venture into the wilderness to submit yourself to this bizarre preaching, you are not likely to notice any difference in either your own life or the life of the community.

Truth hasn't really arrived, in other words.

But when John the Baptist goes on in his remarks to talk about preparing the way of the Lord, and making straight in the desert a highway for God, then he is talking about the hard work of mobilizing people to respond to truth. Now truth is on a highway, moving out of the fringe wilderness into the center of the life of a nation. Truth is coming to your doorstep.

Now God's children, after decades of struggle and suffering, are walking on God's pristine beaches.

But how, in the midst of history, without the benefit of hindsight, do you come upon truth that will liberate people? And perhaps more importantly, how do you organize the life of a community around this new truth? And how do you create a community of faith that actively tries to uncover truth, and to continually reconfigure itself in response?

In an era when we all sense the crowding in upon life of oppressive forces, who is on the scene to lead us? Do we hear the voices of prophetic truth in the halls of Congress or in the boardrooms of America or in the sanctuaries of the religious establishment?

If the status quo that we experience as we confront life in our neighborhood, at our workplace, and through the daily pervasive assault of the media is a status quo of utter confusion, we are tempted to retreat to our church or synagogue on the weekend to find a respite. The last thing we want to hear is a pulpit pronouncement that threatens whatever normalcy remains. In fact, the old political slogan, "A Return to Normalcy," might be a good banner to lead the procession down the aisle when we hear the entrance hymn, "A Mighty Fortress Is Our God."

Unfortunately for those of us who seek such solace, "A Return to Normalcy" is not the banner of the original gospel message. But the Church has often managed to massage the truth into some convoluted conformity to the status quo. Church has become a nostalgic return to the good old days, a celebration of the traditions of our faith that remain a last bulwark against the onslaught of contemporary social change. The traditions that were born out of religious revolution, captured for us in writing on the pages of both the Hebrew Scriptures and the New Testament, have now become the establishment Bible.

That Bible is often brandished by the militant crusaders, the defenders of slavery, and the imperialists who have moved through history to shore up the faith against social change that is generally seen to be inherently threatening.

And some social changes are undeniably threatening. For example, the invasion of urban and suburban neighborhoods by the drug trade is a clear social change. Every sane person wants a respite from the violence of urban America. No one celebrates the number of children born out of wedlock. These realities constitute massive social change during our lifetimes.

In response to these changes, we are tempted to make the Church almost literally a fortress. But that approach fails to recognize that such a reactive Church is more the cause of social upheaval than the antidote. Precisely because the Church has failed to be prophetic, and has failed to mobilize its members and its community around the new possibilities for goodness, the Church has lost its power.

The story of All Saints is the story of a church, deeply rooted in a wonderful tradition, that has mobilized itself around the new possibilities for goodness. And the principal architect of our corporate response to these possibilities is our Rector, George Regas.

This book is the story of this church, and this Rector.

But in order to understand the story, the history of the church that established the foundation for its current greatness must be examined. That prior church had a greatness of its own, of course, just as the one must have that follows upon George's retirement. And the nature of the Christian faith as a faith that enables individuals and societies to walk on God's beaches must be articulated. These are the virgin beaches of personal transformation and social change. The story of All Saints is the evolution of an urban church, called by God to continually reconfigure itself around new possibilities for goodness.

The purpose of Jesus, who is the leader of this Christian faith, was not merely to communicate content, which could have been communicated with more precision without all the grief of the incarnation, but also spirit. What spirit of progressive change do you bring to the status quo of your world? That is forever the key question. And the second is like unto it: How do you organize and empower a community of faith to incarnate this spirit in the midst of your world?

Jesus had to come to live with us to show us who he was, how he inspired people in the most profound sense of that word and how he fought against the status quo of injustice. The specific issues of his time are no longer our issues. If they were our issues, then we would be tolerating slavery, as Jesus did.

But his spirit must be our spirit.

Jesus finds his place at the head of a historic process of reconciliation and liberation. Our task, if we are fearless enough to take up the cause, is to "do greater things" than Jesus by going beyond the issues of first century Palestine and applying the same unquenchable spirit to our own culture.

The spirit of his ministry was the Holy Spirit of revolutionary change.

The gospel was always meant to be the power for change, not the bulwark against change.

But is such a spirit relevant to our day? Can a human institution really engage the seemingly superhuman forces of our culture and actually make a difference?

No. But a human institution—very flawed in many respects—can live out of the resources of the Holy Spirit. And such an institution can't help but make a difference.

Under the leadership of George Regas, and through the witness of All Saints Church, a serious attempt has been made to be faithful to this Holy Spirit. I suppose that nothing more substantial can be said about a man and his congregation. The unfolding drama of the last few decades at 132 North Euclid in Pasadena is simply the story of this faithfulness.

And what a momentous story!

The purpose of this book is not to present the *fait accompli* of a church the way it is supposed to be. The work of the Spirit takes many forms.

But the spirit of faithfulness and the commitment to building a parish is worthy of emulation. And the details of a great ministry are merely illustrative of this faithfulness and this commitment.

The legacy of George Regas is a legacy of allowing the Spirit of Christ to energize a community of faith. A prophetic voice is only a starting point. Building a place in the wilderness of our society where the Spirit of Christ can be brought to bear in such a way as to transform individuals and community—that is the great gift that All Saints Church provides to its members, to Pasadena, and to twentieth century civilization.

This statement is on the one hand grandiose and arrogant. Who are we to think that we could make such an impact on our civilization?

But such a role is precisely what Jesus envisioned for his disciples—the leaven in the lump, the salt of the earth, the city set upon a hill. If we make the statement without any substance, then we are being pompous. If we make the statement and offer some arguable incarnation of it, then we are being faithful.

Read this book, consider this legacy, and judge for yourself. Have lives indeed been transformed? Has society changed to align itself with the supreme reality of Christ's undying love for the world?

If so, then the historic procession with Christ at the head

gathers momentum and invites us to take our place. Our own churches and our own neighborhoods can also be mobilized for transformation and liberation.

If we follow in this line of march, we will be discovering some of God's beaches, where we have never walked before.

The earliest frame church built in 1885 at the northeast corner of Colorado and Garfield.

The old wooden church at 132 N. Euclid, which served the congregation from 1889 to 1923.

Chapter 2

The Heartbeat of a New Parish

SOMETIME AT MIDWEEK during the mid-1950s, Tom Craig stopped by the office at All Saints Church. In that Dwight Eisenhower era just about everyone went to church on Sunday, and Tom was no exception. He had been relocated to the west coast by the Aetna Life Insurance Company, and after settling in Pasadena he sought out the local parish so that he could transfer his membership.

For many white upper middle class Episcopalians, All Saints was the parish of choice in the Diocese of Los Angeles.

Life and worship at All Saints were pleasant and traditional. Pasadena was a wonderful place to live, still the haven for easterners, either for a season or for a lifetime, seeking the warmer climes and the prosperity and the palm trees of Southern California. Since the late 1800s they had come in droves, and the All Saints parish had grown since its modest beginning in 1882, along with the city, and had become the largest Episcopal parish west of the Mississippi River.

Dr. Leslie Learned had reigned at All Saints from 1908 until 1936. "Reign" is an appropriate term. He presided over a "carriage trade" of Episcopalians, mostly conservative and Republican, who gathered for worship in the environment of the Prayer Book and ushers in morning coats. The Vestry, all men, served for life, and they met once a month on the day nearest the full moon, as there were no street lights yet on Euclid Avenue.

Dr. Learned's concept of rule was influenced by his beloved Queen Victoria, she of the mother Church of England. A Union Jack was draped over the lectern once a year to celebrate her birthday. The first section of pews in the church was reserved for the elite pillars of the congregation, who paid $7.50 per month for the privilege, including the cost of engraving their names on their selected seats of worship.

The beautiful Gothic structure that continues to serve All Saints was completed under Dr. Learned's leadership in 1925. The old wooden building on the same site had been outgrown. Dr. Learned insisted that the Tiffany and Maitland Armstrong windows that had been created for the former structure be installed prominently in the new. He hired architects Reginald Johnson, Roland Coate and Gordon Kaufmann, who had to accept that proviso without question.

One would think that it would be a delight to accommodate such beautiful stained glass. But a theological if not architectural problem presented itself. The Maitland Armstrong window over the high altar had been given by a member of a prominent tobacco family, and it memorialized a mother and her three children. The scene was definitely Palestine, a scene you might have created out of felt board figures during a Sunday School class, complete with flowing robes and cherubic faces. But the mother was definitely Mrs. Mary Buchanan Myers, and the little ones were unmistakably the three Myers children.

This all seemed quite proper to Dr. Learned—amiable, beloved, venerable, and pastoral. His theology seldom if ever brought him into conflict with the upper middle class culture of his Pasadena.

The architect received some satisfaction by creating a rood screen, under the cover of theology, that at least partially veiled the offensive stained glass window. Dr. Learned liked the rood screen for theological and some sociological reasons as well—the distance between clergy and laity was preserved and the aloofness of his imperial rectorship reinforced.

Dr. Learned definitely ruled over the Vestry and congregation and overwhelmed any notion of lay empowerment. He had fired one of his assistants for doctrinal variation. The only time politics invaded his pulpit in any challenging way was when he preached against the presidential candidacy of Al Smith, a Roman Catholic, with no objection.

On the social service front, there was the traditional collection of canned goods for the local children's home, and the sewing of clothing and bedding for a favorite mission of Dr. Learned's, located safely in Alaska.

There may have been one Negro family and two Negro women members of the congregation, two ladies who served as housecleaners and cooks for more prominent members of the parish. The Negro ladies sat in the balcony. St. Barnabas parish had been created to serve the few Negro Anglicans in Pasadena, and the general feeling of the time was that St. Barnabas was the appropriate place for such folks, most of whom were domestic workers. The establishment of such a parish was seen to be compassionate, and not racist or malicious.

When a Negro chauffeur arrived with his white employer one Sunday morning at All Saints, an usher turned him away, reportedly, and the white family left also, but there was little fuss or controversy. The newcomer white person simply didn't understand Pasadena's community norms, and the sense of propriety of the transplanted Church of England.

These norms included the reality that Negro families could only use the municipal swimming pool, the Brookside Plunge, one day a week, just before the water was changed and the pool was thoroughly scrubbed.

But the local branch of the National Association for the Advancement of Colored People, led by a Negro physician named Dr. Edna Griffin, brought suit to force the complete sharing and integration of the swimming pool. The suit was filed in 1939, and finally was won in 1945, after which the Brookside Plunge was conveniently closed for two years because of an alleged shortage of revenues and an abundance of repairs.

The Plunge was opened in 1947 to all residents, the same year that a Pasadenan named Jackie Robinson became the first Negro major league baseball player.

Father William Wilkins was the Priest-in-Charge at St. Barnabas beginning in 1933. He participated in this early movement for civil rights as an activist clergyman and president of the NAACP, but without any apparent support from the much more highly regarded All Saints a mile away. Bill Wilkins, in his retirement, would eventually return to Pasadena and serve part time on the staff of George Regas. And Lydia Wilkins, Bill's widow, is a member of All Saints even today.

The Wilkins' experience in Pasadena was a reflection of the times. One of their daughters was sick and needed to be taken to a local hospital. When she arrived, the hospital wouldn't admit her because of her race.

But the hospital hadn't reckoned on the presence in town of Carrie Maude Henderson Paulson. Carrie and her husband had moved to Pasadena from Atlanta in 1916. They eventually raised six children, and their Ludie, who was four at the time of the move, recently passed away in the modest original family homestead on North Mentor Avenue.

The Paulsons were poor, and they never could afford to rent one of the prime pews, but they transferred their membership from St. Luke's in Atlanta to All Saints nonetheless.

Carrie was a Democrat and an activist, one of the few of either at All Saints and one of the few in Pasadena. One of Dr. Learned's deacons would eventually threaten her with excommunication, but not just for being a Democrat. She was simply too outspoken on progressive social issues.

For example, only the boys at All Saints had a choir until Carrie Paulson pressed for the creation of a Girls' Choir. She started and led the Young People's Fellowship, and populated it with her own children.

But these issues were tame compared to the paramount controversy over the rights of Negroes. Ludie remembered going to school one morning in the mid-1930s as her mom sat down to a hot oatmeal breakfast. Carrie's breakfast was interrupted by a phone call that conveyed the news about the Wilkins' daughter being turned away at the hospital. She got on the phone and called everyone in town and everyone at the hospital she could think of. Ensuing phone calls from many aroused parties began to flood the hospital switchboard. Carrie got on the Red Line streetcar near her home, the one that the family always took to church, and went to see city and hospital officials in person.

By the time Ludie arrived home from school late that afternoon, the untouched oatmeal had grown cold on the dining room table. But Alfreda Wilkins had been admitted to the hospital.

Bill and Lydia Wilkins' best friends in those days were Edna and Ernest Banks. They went to St. Barnabas together, and later joined All Saints after Bill's retirement and after such integration became more acceptable. In the 1930s Ernest and Edna had a race-related experience in their own family.

Their daughter Lois was nine and attended public school. During the summer the leader of the local Young Women's Christian Association invited girls to come to the Y for games and fun. Little Lois went along. Nothing was said about whites only.

When Lois entered the historic YWCA building that still stands at the corner of Marengo and Holly in Pasadena, she was told that she could play ping-pong but not go in the pool.

Lois called home in confusion and distress. Edna Banks never looked for trouble, but when she heard her daughter weeping over the phone she went into action. She spoke with Miss Day, the director of the Y program and the daughter of the local prominent Methodist minister.

Miss Day politely and patiently explained the ping-pong option, but Edna responded that this wasn't about ping-pong. It was about the rights of her child, and the hurt that had been inflicted.

Edna was a collector for the local Community Chest, which supported the Y and other charities, supposedly without regard to race. So she set up a meeting of the Community Chest and YWCA officials, at which time it was explained to her that the pool at the YWCA was separately and privately endowed, hence the legitimacy of the discrimination, in honor of the wishes of the benefactor.

Such technical niceties made no impression on Edna Banks, and her arguments and persistence eventually held sway. Daughter Lois was admitted to the YWCA pool.

The Diocese of Los Angeles had an Episcopal Church Camp named Camp Stevens, in honor of the Diocesan Bishop. Bishop W. Bertrand Stevens visited St. Barnabas one day and was asked a question by Lydia Wilkins.

"Can our children attend your camp?" The Bishop was puffing on a cigar that he reportedly almost swallowed. But he recovered nicely and responded, "There is no reason why they can't go."

The summer immediately following, the two children of Bill and Lydia Wilkins and the two children of Ernest and Edna Banks became the first of the Negro race to attend the mountain camp. Alfreda Wilkins wrote home during that momentous week: "Bishop Stevens preached last night and he did right well!"

Now I know we have left poor Tom Craig at the beginning of this chapter standing in the All Saints office at midweek. We have left him there for a reason, and we will rescue him shortly, but first let us continue our summary of life at All Saints leading up to Tom Craig's arrival.

Dr. John Frank Scott came from Columbus, Ohio, in 1936, with his wife, Millie, to serve as the Rector at All Saints. They stayed until his retirement in 1957. Dr. Learned had retired after a distinguished three decades of service. But his service was more distinguished for who he was—his integrity and his bearing—than for his accomplishments.

Dr. Scott would become just as beloved and just as venerable during his long tenure, but he would lead the church gradually in some new directions. And, of course, times changed in Pasadena. The city was becoming more populous and less homogeneous. Dr. Scott regretted the influx of businesses spilling over from Los Angeles ten miles to the west, but Pasadena was becoming less of an upper middle class bedroom community. When he gave his successor, John Burt, an automobile tour of the city in 1957, his yearning for the "good old days" was apparent.

Frank Scott would not exhibit the challenging leadership and the dramatic flair of John Burt or George Regas after him; he was quiet and pastoral. But he moved the church in some important ways that laid the foundation for later progress.

He did away with the rented pews, and with that aristocratic symbolism. He at least partially moved the Vestry away from its elitism by allowing for a Junior Vestry, younger members of the parish, who sat around the perimeter of the Vestry meetings and eventually began to assert a more democratic upstart leadership style.

A Parish Board of Education and a Laymen's League were formed. The communication process was opened up by the publication of a monthly bulletin. Dr. Scott's sermons, like Dr. Learned's before him, were broadcast over the airwaves and summarized in the Monday morning *Pasadena Star-News*.

And Dr. Scott developed a much more progressive reputation in the community for himself and for the parish. Early in World War II, he opposed the relocation of the Japanese-Americans, many of whom lived in Pasadena. When the trains left the local Santa Fe station, Dr. Scott showed up to protest. A member of the parish, retired Missionary Bishop of North Tokyo Charles Reifsnider, carried on a regular pastoral ministry to the Nisei relocated to the nearby Santa Anita Race Track stables.

Frank Scott supported the creation of the United Nations, which was controversial and enlightened for his time and place. He also believed in individual members of the congregation serving the wider community through their volunteer efforts.

And finally, to Dr. Scott's credit, he wished that someone would throw a rock through that stained glass window above the altar.

Generally the parish became more active and slightly more heterogeneous. It was still largely concerned only with its internal affairs when John Burt arrived, but there were now many more communicants added to the 1,685 that Dr. Scott had inherited.

Both Dr. Learned and Dr. Scott were capable pastors and well-loved by their congregations. Their kind of consistent leadership created a place of prominence in Pasadena for themselves and for All Saints Church.

They presided over a healthy and prosperous parish, established a laudable presence in the community, and generally turned over to John Burt in 1957 an enviable place for a young minister to make his mark. Although John had not heard of

All Saints during his years at Virginia Seminary and at his parish in Youngstown, Ohio, he would recall that Dr. Eugene Carson Blake, formerly pastor at Pasadena Presbyterian Church, and later head of the World Council of Churches, had told him that All Saints was a "plum ripe for the picking."

The leadership of John Burt's predecessors had attracted some wonderful families to the parish. Hidden in among the members were some lay people waiting to tackle the challenges of the tumultuous post-Eisenhower years. Several of the brightest of them would drop their children off at Sunday School and walk down the street to Thrifty's Drugstore, which had a lunch counter in those days, for food and fellowship during the educational hour. They were yearning, perhaps without knowing it, for a new kind of leadership.

John Burt's arrival would be a turning point in the style and substance of the parish. He would harness the energy of aggressive laypeople like Tom Craig.

When Tom arrived at midweek, a few years before Frank Scott's retirement, he couldn't find a pledge card to fill out. So the parish secretary had to create one for the occasion. Pledges were taken in via a postcard response in the fall. The budget was $70,000 a year.

The budget was set and the fall date for pledging hadn't arrived, and Tom Craig had the audacity to interrupt this casual approach with an insistence on making a financial commitment, off-season.

The fact that his presence in the parish office at midweek was so intrusive speaks volumes about the laid-back atmosphere at All Saints. Pledging was nominal, and visits by laypeople, except for Sunday morning, were extraordinary.

Tom Craig had made an impact on his new parish by making, as a newcomer, one of the largest pledges of any parishioner. That pledge had a spiritual, as well as a financial, bearing on the future of All Saints.

All Saints was ready for change. Tom Craig became the Senior Warden within a few years, and he led the Search Committee of the Vestry to find a replacement for Frank Scott. Eventually Tom came calling on John Burt, who was the third choice in the search process—just as Frank Scott had been a third choice in 1936 and just as George Regas would be in 1967.

People like Tom Craig represented the heartbeat of a new parish—one that would build on the foundation established by Leslie Learned and Frank Scott, one that would engage the history and the contemporary realities of life in the city of Pasadena, and one that would capture the yearning of a new breed of parishioners.

John Burt would come to merge his energy and vision with theirs.

The current Gothic structure consecrated in 1925.

Chapter 3

The Church as an Outpost

JOHN BURT had already gotten into some political hot water at his post in Youngstown, Ohio. He had worked to allow Negroes in community swimming pools, and against the censorship of books at the local library. He had become a founding president of the Youngstown branch of the American Civil Liberties Union. And in Ohio Diocesan affairs, he was a leading force in social justice ministries.

His reputation raised a few eyebrows at All Saints, prior to his coming. He had a notable doubter on the Vestry in the very influential person of Reese Taylor, the head of the Union Oil Company. Mr. Taylor thought the ACLU was Communist, so at his urging a member of the Vestry who was a personal friend of J. Edgar Hoover wrote to find out if the Federal Bureau of Investigation had a file on Mr. Burt. The answer came back in the negative.

John had insisted that if he were to come across country with his wife Martha and their four daughters, ages two through eight, he would need a unanimous vote from the Vestry. The majority who were strongly in favor prevailed upon Reese Taylor to abstain, so the vote could be technically unanimous, and the Burts arrived in January of 1957.

People began to take All Saints more seriously as a force within the community. Within the church people like Tom Craig went to work to make the parish operate in a more business-like fashion. Pledge cards became available year-round. The bookkeeping system was upgraded. A modernized phone system was installed. Regular weekly staff meetings were held. The Vestry was set up on a rotating basis, so that fresh ideas would bubble up to empower the parish. And some of these ideas would come from women! There was a bit more democracy and a bit less hierarchy. More of the young leaders began to take charge, responding to the more activist vision of the church that John Burt had imported.

John had inherited a music program that operated within the parish like a separate empire. The choir was mostly loyal to their winsome director, but John found his approach to music quite unsatisfactory, and his inability to see this realm as part of the larger liturgical design intolerable. The director played much of the more familiar classical music "by ear," leaving out parts that he was unable to play. John began to involve himself in planning the liturgy, a domain that had been reserved in the All Saints tradition for the music director alone.

During one exchange in the Rector's office over the liturgy, the music director hastily said that perhaps he should just resign, if his talents weren't appreciated. John politely agreed. And when the director came back shortly to undo the damage of his emotional outburst, John firmly allowed that the resignation had already been accepted, and there was no need to renegotiate.

So John had his opportunity to bring in a choir director and organist of his own choosing, a musical whiz named Bill MacGowan who gave new energy to liturgy and worship at All Saints. The church has never been the same since, and has never retreated from its commitment to excellence and creativity in music.

A new choir was formed; special programs were offered.

Exciting music highlighted the Sunday morning services, often embellished by instrumentalists. Bill MacGowan launched a tradition that was strengthened under a succession of outstanding church musicians, continuing to the present day.

All of these changes and more to come had a spiritual dimension. One may think that there is nothing spiritual about installing a modern phone system, having pledge cards available year 'round, or being able to play a Mendelssohn piece without omitting the parts that are too difficult. One would be very mistaken.

When people take the church seriously they give it their meticulous attention. Sloppiness is not a Christian virtue. The occasional spontaneity of the movement of the Holy Spirit arises out of intense preparation. The prophetic voice in the wilderness may come without corporate intentionality, but preparing in the desert a highway for God is a massive logistical undertaking.

John Burt knew that liturgy could transport a congregation into a realm of greater spiritual possibilities, that the availability of pledge cards could jumpstart renewal in the life of an individual or a community. These were not incidental to the Kingdom of God.

Not everyone in John Burt's day agreed. At an early Vestry meeting John suggested that the parish might create a ten-year plan complete with goals and strategies. Such an approach was unheard of. A Vestry member asked how such a plan might be useful.

"We might find ways to enhance our ministry," John replied.

"Like what ways?" responded the unimpressed Vestryman.

"Well, we might find, for example, that we need to provide specialized psychological counseling for troubled people," said John, quickly searching his mind for what he thought would be a non-controversial illustration.

"Sounds like a pretty left-wing idea to me," came the reply.

And so the discussion went. The fact that Burt won the vote of the Vestry on the issue is not as revealing as the fact that such questions could legitimately be raised by a lay leader of the church. If the church is just an incidental nicety, you don't need ten-year plans. You just need to play that little game you played as a child when you cupped your hands and recited:

"Here is the church and here is the steeple; open the door and see all the people!"

During the 1950s attending church had become the accepted thing to do on Sunday mornings, especially for young families with growing children. Citizens trusted their governmental leaders and looked to Ozzie and Harriet Nelson for inspiration. Not many people expected their lives to be transformed, or the power of the gospel to be unleashed within a community.

But John Burt looked at the community and saw a more dramatic role for All Saints, consistent with his understanding of the Spirit of Christ. He expected people in his parish to take their faith seriously and apply it to those issues they might otherwise consider to be secular and out of bounds.

John's style was not to go on a one-man reactive crusade on any one issue. He was more thoughtful and incremental. He did bring some issues to the attention of the parish, however.

The west coast branch of the John Birch Society was headquartered in nearby San Marino, with the avowed intent to ferret out Communists and other social radicals from places of influence—from government and the entertainment industry in particular. Children were still being denied equal opportunity because of the color of their skin. Hardworking farmworkers in California could not afford to feed their own families. Fair housing was little more than a slogan.

John illustrated his sermons with references to these and other social conditions of the day. He wrote a weekly column in the church bulletin that often focused on ways for Christians to work for a more just society. And he created an Adult Forum on Sunday mornings to voice his own views and to bring in outside experts to present sometimes controversial opinions to the parish.

A new spirit of inquiry and engagement began to take hold at All Saints.

And John Burt became a model of community witness. Early on he threw himself into the work of the Pasadena Council of Churches and the Pasadena Community Planning Council, becoming the president of each in short order. They became vehicles for a witness about family planning, race relations, equal opportunity for jobs and housing, services for the mentally ill, and school integration.

The issue of race relations was especially sensitive in Southern California. Martin Luther King, Jr., was rising in prominence nationally, and John chaired events in Los Angeles that brought him to town to speak. He occasionally took parishioners to participate in rallies.

All of this activity brought a visit from three esteemed members of the Vestry who thought the Rector was spending too much time in the pulpit talking about race. John listened intently to their complaints. They asked him to ease up on the rhetoric. They themselves were clearly not racists—that would have made their plea easy to reject. They thought it acceptable, though a bit embarrassing, that John was active in the community. But they wanted him to allow for more congeniality and tranquility on Sunday mornings without the racial justice harangues.

John got the threesome to agree that the pulpit would, of course, always be free. No one could control the content of the sermon other than the preacher in response to the Spirit of God and the word of God.

"Yes, of course, we don't want to infringe on the freedom of the pulpit. We are good friends, and just trying to give you some advice," they said.

John knew they were loyal churchmen. One had founded the Pasadena Council on Alcoholism and a chapter of the United Nations Association. Another was the driving force behind the Episcopal Home for the Aged. John took them and their concerns seriously, and they were honored by that.

During the ensuing week John took out all his recent sermons and carefully reviewed them to see how much he had been pounding on one theme. When the group came back together, they were impressed that John had done his homework, but surprised that he felt their complaints were overstated. After a comprehensive review, John was shocked that he was spending so little time on the issue of race relations. He promised to do more. All of the three grumbled but remained loyal to his leadership.

The important point is not whether one is for or against a specific issue. The point has to do with a view of the Church that is dramatically different from the tradition of All Saints prevalent up through the 1950s. The Church is to be a social leaven, a change agent in society.

John's three visitors wanted their church to be a fortress against the rising tide of social unrest, rather than an outpost in the midst of it. A fortress is a safeguard against the encroachment of unwelcome forces; an outpost is a springboard from which those forces may be challenged and converted.

The issue of individual renewal is tied inextricably to the engagement of the world and the pursuit of social justice. And furthermore, the mobilization of a parish for pastoral care, liturgical excellence, organizational competence, and educational nurture is all of a piece with individual and communal transformation.

All Saints under the leadership of John Burt was slowly becoming a force in all of these areas. An intangible expectation seemed to challenge and woo people to the serious pursuit of discipleship. And people were coming to John's side with their own creative offerings.

Bob Morton, for example, had caught a vision that could not be contained by the modest annual church budget of about $95,000. Bob had been confirmed one Sunday and had been proposed for the Vestry soon thereafter because of his aggressive leadership qualities. He didn't have all of his theology in order, however.

In response to the invitation to join the Vestry, he asked, "Do I have to believe in God?"

"Well, do you wish there were a God?" the Rector asked.

"Yes."

"Then pretend it is so and hope it is so and act as if it's true. And welcome to the Vestry!"

Even under the previous "church as a fortress" leadership of Dr. Learned and Dr. Scott, the doctrinal litmus test for lay leadership was minimal. Under John Burt and later George Regas, the concept of the spiritual journey was all important. To be on the journey was a requirement; to have arrived at some theological way station of orthodox belief was not.

So Bob Morton under John Burt came to the fore and brashly asserted that he wanted to lead an every-member canvass. That was an especially bold request, since All Saints had never had one.

But Bob conducted a stewardship drive that was worthy of a church that took itself seriously. John Burt initially was skeptical of the goal of doubling the annual giving in one year. Bob probably hadn't heard of the biblical tithe, but he thought that people ought to give to the church at least as much as they spent on cigarettes. That sounded biblical enough to him. Maybe that was the secret meaning behind the high altar window. And he knew in his heart that people of substantial means ought to be giving more than $50 a year to their church. He and a cadre of lay leaders invaded the homes of parishioners and told them so. And he achieved a one-year jump of 96 percent in the annual pledging!

Liz Morton, Bob's wife, was drawn into the social justice fray when she asked to ride with the Burts to attend a "Rally for Freedom" for Martin Luther King, Jr., at Los Angeles' old Wrigley Field. John and Martha and Liz were about the only whites in a throng of over 35,000. Liz became a convert. She would become, at the invitation of George Regas in 1975, the first woman Senior Warden at All Saints, and possibly in the nation.

When you win the allegiance of people like Bob and Liz Morton, along with many others, you have the makings of a powerful parish.

The Farmworkers Union was emerging in California under the charismatic leadership of Cesar Chavez, and John Burt publicly identified himself with their cause. The All Saints membership included some of the largest agribusiness interests in the world. They were not inclined to be friendly toward the demands of the farmworkers.

Chavez came at John's invitation to an All Saints' Adult Forum. He told his compelling story of the personal struggle for dignity and decency.

John knew that Robert Rowan was the president of the Republican Party in California and a powerful real estate tycoon, but what he didn't know was that much of Rowan's personal real estate holdings consisted of farmland. He would soon find out. Rowan and Burt sat on a park bench and spent a morning discussing their differences. The most important part of the conversation went something like this, according to John's recollection:

"Bob, if you were a farmworker, working on one of your farms, do you think you would make enough money to feed and house your family, and to have a refrigerator to store milk for your children?"

Robert Rowan thought for a moment and responded, "No, John, I guess I wouldn't." The two forged a relationship of great mutual respect, despite some ongoing differences.

Overriding all the differences among many parishioners was a sense of pastoral love and nurture. That covered a multitude of sins that people otherwise would have laid at the doorstep of John Burt. And in addition to that spiritual quality that was a hallmark of his ministry, John had the good fortune and good sense to persuade a senior priest named Sidney Sweet to assist him through almost all of his ten years as All Saints' Rector.

Sidney Sweet, 72 years old at the time, was as lovable and loyal as they come. He had recently retired as Dean of Christ Church Cathedral in St. Louis, had been John Burt's mentor while John served an internship in St. Louis years earlier, and had even introduced John to parishioner Martha Miller, who would later become Martha Burt.

If some people were suspicious of John and his social and political positions, they couldn't help having complete trust in Sidney. And Sidney was a listener even more than John was. He extracted the venom from people and replaced it with tolerance for John, if not outright devotion. Beneath the genuine friendliness and inclusivity of Sidney was a liberal heart as great as that of any leader in the Episcopal Church during the first half of the twentieth century. John could find encouragement in Sidney's counsel, at the same time that

Sidney, without duplicity, could shepherd the less enthusiastic members into a constructive relationship with their parish and their Rector.

These critics generally fell into several different categories. One group took exception to particular stands on certain issues. The growers in the congregation didn't care for some of Burt's positions on farmworkers' rights, for example. Sometimes these differences could be tolerated in the context of a general support for the overall ministry. In other cases, the critics perceived their differences to be so fundamental that people left the parish. As far as John was concerned, his own attitude toward critics remained positive, and their departure was always painful.

In John Burt's day, parishioners could more easily compartmentalize the Rector as a separate entity from the church. They would read in the newspapers about John's convening a rally called the Town Meeting for Democracy at the Shrine Auditorium in Los Angeles. Rod Serling was there. Senator Eugene McCarthy, a Democrat, and Senator Clifford Case, a Republican, were among the speakers. President John F. Kennedy wired his support.

All this effort was designed to rebuke the upsurge of the extreme right in its threat to traditional American freedoms. Some members of All Saints were unsympathetic with John's position. They naturally would wince when they saw their Rector leading their opposition.

But at least there was not an official All Saints' mobilization for the Town Meeting for Democracy. John wasn't leading an All Saints parade or convening a parish committee. He was simply exercising his conscience as a community leader, and using his bully pulpit, or more often his bully bulletin column, to bring the issue to the attention of his parish and the general public.

So people who disagreed with the Rector on a particular issue at least felt they weren't in opposition to their church, because John never sought the official blessing of the Vestry for his community involvements, and he never unilaterally declared an All Saints position.

Of course, such a compartmentalization of roles can never be airtight. And in all these social causes other parishioners would pop up as leaders or participants, often with John's encouragement. So the church began to receive a certain notoriety.

The fact that John Burt's home, the Rectory no less, was the site of a middle of the night detonation of some sort just prior to the Town Meeting for Democracy, strengthened the sense of some in the community that Burt was a different kind of Rector. No one would have responded to Dr. Learned or Dr. Scott in such a way. On the night of the rally, police had to protect the Rectory so that Martha could go to the Shrine Auditorium, knowing that the four young Burt daughters would be safe at home.

Another group of discontented parishioners was not aroused by any isolated Burt provocation. But they saw their church slipping away from them. The nature of the parish was changing, and the aura of All Saints as a center of calm and a safeguard against the vicissitudes of culture was shifting.

John often preached on the concept of the servants of God becoming of necessity the servants of community. And he practiced what he preached. People from All Saints had always been in places of power in government and commerce in the Los Angeles area. Now these same people, and others without the trappings of influence, were becoming the social reformers of Pasadena. The church was a springboard for their involvement in a host of causes. At the beginning of each Vestry meeting, John would pass around a list of parishioners and the responsibilities they had accepted to serve in a host of civic and social welfare roles.

John had written about his goals for All Saints that he wanted to "lift up the Christian faith and make it relevant to problems of daily living as part of the worldwide Anglican communion open to all races." The statement seemed mild in the context of polite Christianity, but in the context of the Church as an outpost, in the midst of the turmoil of the 1960s, the statement signalled a shift in emphasis that troubled some and attracted others.

People were taking the church seriously. People were coming out of the church to challenge the status quo and engage in moral discourse on the "secular" issues of the day. Some of God's beaches began to open up to farmworkers and women and Negroes. Some parishioners retreated from this turn of events. And others rejoiced.

Chapter 4

Gathering the Faithful

PEOPLE IN THE JOHN BURT ERA began to identify All Saints with community causes. Some who were used to a different kind of church drifted away. But others in the community who ordinarily had little use for religion came by for a dose.

Adele Barnes had been attending St. Mark's Church just a few blocks from her home in Altadena. She had come to the Pasadena area after graduating from Radcliffe College and working for women's suffrage for a few years, alongside her mother, father and sister. When I interviewed Adele, now 101 years old, we were sitting in the same living room where she had been introduced to Hobert Barnes for the first time in 1922. They were married in 1926. She had worked in the social welfare field on behalf of immigrant women and unwed mothers.

After a long and distinguished professional career, Adele had a bit of trouble going to a church, no matter how convenient, where she was continually put down as a second class citizen. Her Rector at St. Mark's was "biblically" opposed to women having any leadership role in the church.

Adele had worked with John Burt in various community activities such as the Council of Churches and the Community Planning Council. They were comrades in arms for farmworkers and school integration. So it was natural for her to make her way to All Saints.

John Burt was committed to making changes in church and society that would give women a greater opportunity to participate. In 1964, when he was president of the Diocesan Standing Committee, John led the successful battle in diocesan convention to change the canons to permit persons of either sex to serve in elected lay posts. This victory, in turn, made it possible for All Saints to elect Ruth Ewing to the Vestry in 1966.

John had also been part of a lobbying effort at the General Convention in 1964, campaigning to make women eligible for elective posts in the leadership of the national church. Everything is relative, of course, and especially on the social justice scene there is a time for pragmatism and compromise. Not every issue at the moment of engagement is clear. So the forces that were proposing the seating of the woman delegate from the Diocese of Missouri were quite content to allow that women still had their place, not quite on a par with men. The statement was made on the convention floor: "If you seat a woman at convention, next she'll be celebrating the eucharist."

But John was prepared with the planned response to this anticipated strategy. "No self-respecting woman would ever want to be a priest," he replied.

So this was the social activist hero who won the allegiance of people like Adele Barnes. She came, along with a rising tide of others who were looking for a church that stood for something they believed in.

But people such as Adele were not just one-note crusaders for a specific issue. Adele wanted to help John build a parish. Dr. Scott had succeeded in a grand way in gathering the flock. Now with more significant issues at stake, there was even more reason to strengthen the infrastructure of the church.

So on Sunday mornings Adele found herself proactively greeting newcomers on the lawn. In a church with so many members, Adele had trouble identifying visitors with certainty. So she would approach a prospect with the innocuous statement: "Wasn't that one of the best sermons he's ever preached?"

If he or she responded, "I don't know. I never heard him preach before," Adele would have her opportunity to introduce the person to the Rector, and to the ongoing life of the parish.

Some who were attracted to All Saints were current members who were simply energized in a new way. The Thrifty's Drugstore contingent and the parents who were in the habit of dropping their children off for Sunday School were now more apt to stay for a sermon or Adult Forum.

Jim and Harriet Fullerton, for example, had been coming on Christmas and Easter since 1951. On other Sundays Jim would sit in the parking lot and read the Sunday paper, or adjourn to Thrifty's for an ice cream cone. One Sunday when the paper had been left inadvertently at home, Jim innocently wandered into the service. Upon leaving, he made the mistake of complimenting John on an especially thoughtful sermon. To which John replied, "Jim, we have wonderful sermons every Sunday!"

Jim and Harriet began to attend regularly, and they eventually became parish-builders as well. Jim's strength was in stewardship, and he teamed up with his friend Bob Morton to transform stewardship campaigns into serious challenges to people's pocketbooks and faith.

One other person of note who was attracted to All Saints in those days was a feisty little woman named Mara Moser. She was an acquaintance of Adele Barnes and John Burt as a member of the Christian Life and Work dinners that the Pasadena Council of Churches was sponsoring.

Mara had a cause, and she was unapologetic about bringing it up at every opportunity. She cared about the families left behind when a member of the family, usually the husband, went to prison.

In those days the local daily, the *Pasadena Star-News*, published the names and addresses of those who had been convicted and sentenced. Mara was a foot soldier for relief. She walked to the identified home and offered to be of help. Mara had a simple Quaker belief in the ministry of service.

Mara's combative style was a nice complement to John's more pastoral approach. She marched into his office one day to ask, "What's the matter with your church?"

"What do you mean, what's the matter?" said John, a bit taken aback.

"Don't you know that breadwinners are going off to prison and leaving behind neglected children and distraught mothers, right here within a few blocks of your congregation?"

John steered the conversation in a constructive direction, and Mara found herself dubbed an All Saints' "Friendly Visitor." She reported to John regularly on her successes and failures. She raised a little money from him and others to supply special needs of the families who welcomed her. Not all did, of course. When a surprised mother asked her how she possibly thought she could help, Mara peered through the closed screen door and said she saw some dishes in the kitchen sink that needed washing.

She was viewed with suspicion by some of the families who told her to mind her own business, and by some on the All Saints Vestry who wondered what this renegade woman was getting the church involved in. But John allayed their fears and most thought she was probably harmless. Some were just a little nervous when they heard that Mara had spoken at a dinner meeting to raise consciousness and in the process raised her skirt and said, "What do I have to do, a strip tease, to get your support for the needs of the families of prisoners?"

The abiding sense of church passivity continued to erode under the influence of people such as Mara and scores of others who saw the church as a rallying point and not just as a retreat center. Walter Shatford, an early crusader for school integration, widely regarded as a "pinko" cause, became a member. People were viewing All Saints Church with greater respect as a player in community affairs, and they were taking their faith more seriously as an avenue for personal renewal.

In 1965 a historic opportunity for church expansion arose which crystallized the debate about the future direction of All Saints. The property just north of the parish became available, and John Burt and others on the Vestry, especially the younger visionary members, wanted to buy it.

The church had an endowment fund of $212,000. This could be used for a down payment, and the church could take on a mortgage to be paid off out of operating funds. But a senior member of the Vestry, a judge, was adamantly opposed.

"Why do we need a church school building beyond what we already have? Can't we get along with the parking that's already available? The church is not in the real estate business."

John decided to postpone the Vestry decision for a month in deference to the judge's complaints, although he risked losing the property in doing so. During that month John took a lot of Vestry people to lunch to convince them of his earnestness and of the need to add a Church School wing. Even the judge softened his outright opposition. The next month the Vestry decided to proceed with the purchase, and today Scott Hall (named after the former Rector), a weekday Children's Center, and the prospect of even further expansion are a testimony to their wisdom.

In his final report to the parish, John would cite the acquisition of the 76,281 square feet of land as "our most obvious achievement in my ten years."

John Burt had one other involvement of note relating to a former Rector. Kenneth Learned, the son of Leslie, was a telephone company executive, a staunch Republican, and the Junior Warden of the Vestry. Kenneth came to John in early 1965 and asked if he intended to go on the Montgomery to Selma march with Martin Luther King, Jr.

John had indeed thought about going. What did Kenneth have in mind? Did he want to object to what the Rector did with his time? Did he recoil from the idea of another picture in the local paper of the meddling priest in Alabama smiling beneath a picket sign. Did he fear for his Rector's safety or sanity?

None of the above. Kenneth wanted to go! John was shocked.

"Would you go, even if I didn't?" John asked.

"Yes, I believe I would."

"Then you go without me and represent the parish, and tell us about your experience when you return."

John knew that Kenneth's going on his own would be a more powerful lay witness than another predictable excursion by the Rector, having twisted the arm of yet another lay person to accompany him.

When Kenneth returned, along with his wife, Dorothy, and five other parishioners who had joined them, he was a changed man. He spoke at the Adult Forum with a sense of energy and spiritual renewal that was uncharacteristic. And he admitted, "My father didn't do it this way."

In some arenas John Burt didn't succeed so handsomely with his Vestry. He ran up against the old bugaboo of that sacrilegious stained glass window above the high altar.

John had once called the Vestry into session in the front rows of the church so that they could hear the true story behind the creation of the masterpiece. Bob Morton, for one, was shocked to learn that the mother and her trinity of little angels did not depict some biblical epic that had inspired the faith of the church for millennia, and certainly his own. He complained that his faith had been destroyed by John's revelation, and Bob had precious little faith in any orthodox sense in the first place.

But the Vestry, while ambivalent about the history of the window, did not see any realistic alternative. And so the window remains to this day, eliciting the naive devotion of thousands.

John's only other opportunity for relief regarding the window came when a miscreant youth group member was found one afternoon in the balcony of the church with a BB gun, shooting out the lights of the chandeliers. When John was summoned from his office across the lawn by a frantic custodian, John's heart momentarily leapt within him. Perhaps an errant pellet would find its way to some vulnerable point above the altar and the whole window would come crashing down.

But John Burt at the end of his tenure had nonetheless accomplished a great deal. In his very first sermon in Pasadena he had expressed a four-fold hope, that All Saints would "produce specialists in the things of the Spirit; become a training center in moral discipline; send forth into the life of the community, state, nation and world bold and fervent witnesses for Christian truth; and be for those who come within its fellowship a Resurrection Center." He left for his successor a church that had reached these plateaus and that was ready to evolve to an even higher level of greatness.

John Burt moved on from All Saints to become the Bishop

of Ohio in 1967. A few in the parish, and a few who had withdrawn, breathed a sigh of relief at John's departure. "Now we can get back to the good old days," was the sentiment of some.

Ken Rhodes, who had chaired the committee to purchase the new $95,000 Schlicker organ as well as the committee to build Scott Hall, was named chair of a search committee for a new Rector. As part of the process, this committee circulated a questionnaire to the parish. "What kind of a Rector and what kind of a church do you want?"

The results were overwhelming and surprising. People wanted more of the same. They wanted a prophetic church with a mission for personal and social renewal.

The eucharist at the center of parish life and ministry.

Chapter 5

A Regimen for Renewal

A GREAT ARTIST was once confronted by an admirer with the question, "Tell me what this painting means."

The artist replied, "If I could tell you what it means, I would not have had to paint it."

To capture the essence of the last 28 years at All Saints under the leadership of George Regas is like trying to explain the meaning of a great work of art. I, for one, have worshiped and worked at All Saints in a very intimate way for 20 years. If I could tell the reader what the experience has meant, I would not have had to live it. And that would be a great artistic loss.

The opportunity exists simply to summarize the considerable efforts that have made All Saints a model for urban ministry. But the life of All Saints is more than just a compilation of outreach programs. The internal life of the church, even though it has a lower profile in the wider community, is just as important to what makes All Saints a great parish. This parish infrastructure of worship and spiritual formation, of Christian education and pastoral care, and of stewardship and administration, is the foundation of all that the church accomplishes.

All Saints is known for its activism. But its activism is rooted in the internal life of the parish. Likewise, spiritual nurture doesn't take place in a setting that is chronologically or geographically distinct from the many ways that the parish reaches out to its neighbors. People aren't transformed and renewed Sunday morning so that they can go out and serve the community during the rest of the week. This is a popular compartmentalization of faith that doesn't hold sway in All Saints' experience.

When a volunteer is serving a sandwich to a hungry neighbor at Union Station, the drop-in hospitality center that All Saints began in 1973, that is a spiritual growth experience. That is a communion with God experience. That is an experience of personal renewal.

And when a parishioner is sharing in the eucharist on Sunday morning, the poor of Union Station invade that sacred moment with their symbolic (and sometimes real) presence. The eucharist is a celebration of the healing of a broken world. The sufficiency of Christ embraces all of God's children as we bring them to the holy feast in our consciousness and commitment.

This synergy of worship and action is perhaps the most powerful component of the ministry of George Regas. The phrase "God is in the work" is a well-known concept among the clergy and staff and lay leadership of All Saints Church. The people in the pew and on the fringes of parish life also participate in this truth.

To relate the story of this work is to relate the story of the man most responsible for what All Saints Church is today: Dr. George Frank Regas.

George was born of Greek immigrant parents in Knoxville, Tennessee, in 1930. His father began a restaurant that remains to this day the pride of Knoxville—the Regas Restaurant, managed by brother Bill. Father Frank was a self-made man and a stereotypical immigrant success story. He loved his new country and his work. George veered toward the priesthood, to his father's dismay. But he did follow in the family tradition of ambition and achievement.

George also absorbed a compassionate spirit from his earliest days, when the restaurant was always accessible to those who had no food and no money. The Regas' family table, especially at the holidays, frequently included one or two guests who had no other family or resources.

George's mother passed away when he was five, and his father died before he entered seminary. But George still carries in his person a strong family loyalty, and a desire to succeed with parents who did not live to witness any of his career accomplishments.

After graduating from Episcopal Divinity School in Cambridge, Massachusetts, in 1956, George proceeded to doctoral studies in New Testament with Bishop John A. T. Robinson in Cambridge, England. The liberal Robinson would become a lifelong friend and mentor. He taught George to hold fast to the center of faith—allegiance to Christ—but to be open and flexible at the edges, where doctrines abound that may help us to love God, but which cannot be allowed to become God.

George's favorite story to illustrate the point is the occasion when he was driving by the Miramar Hotel south of Santa Barbara just prior to Easter. A sign on the marquee asked in bold letters: "Do you have your Easter reservations?" He said to himself, "Do I ever!"

George has a few Christmas and Easter and in-between reservations. But those who scoff and suggest that these reservations about orthodox Christian doctrine might get in the way of devotion to Christ don't understand George Regas in the least. He is a living example that an open-ended and intellectually honest faith can still move mountains.

John Robinson also confirmed George's inclination to believe that the union of worship with the ministry of healing the world makes for authentic Christianity.

George's studies in England were interrupted by illness. (He would complete his doctorate later at the School of Theology at Claremont, California.) In 1957 he became the Vicar of a small congregation in Pulaski, Tennessee, not far from the place where the Ku Klux Klan was organized. In 1960 he became the Rector of Grace Church in Nyack, New York, and in 1967, at the age of 36, he was summoned to Pasadena.

Early on in his career, long before he had heard of All Saints Church, some disciplines were in place that would empower George's ministry.

The principal discipline has to do with a time alone each weekday morning, and all day on Thursday. George's study is a very sacred place. In my own tenure at All Saints, I believe I have knocked on the study door one time, with fear and trembling. It is a place tucked away in a far corner of the second story of the Parish House, and after the disastrous Parish House fire in 1976, it was the only item on George's non-negotiable list for rebuilding. The preservation of this time and place is the greatest gift George can offer to his staff and parishioners.

1. The regimen begins with the lectionary scripture readings assigned for the day.

2. Then a time of contemplation with as blank a consciousness as is humanly possible follows.

3. Then George thinks in categories, focusing on the people who are part of the ministry: the prayer list, the pledge list, the Vestry, the picture directory of the parish. "Who are these people? What is God telling me about them? What is supposed to happen in our interaction?" Many of George's people and pastoral skills, and his uncanny knack for redemptive relationships flow out of this time.

4. Then George lets the world into his consciousness in a deliberate way. The morning paper has been digested. "What

is happening around the globe and in our community? What is the role of the church?" Much of the prophetic ministry flows out of these considerations.

5. And finally, "What is the day's agenda?" George reviews the calendar of meetings and appointments, clarifies the goals for each encounter, and asks God's guidance and blessing.

The outline for this approach to ministry and to life was present in Pulaski and in Nyack, so that by the time the pressures of the Pasadena post threatened to pull George in many uncoordinated directions, the commitment to these morning times was already unshakable. The Rector and the congregation would be renewed by this discipline for many years.

With regard to the prophetic ministry, and the persistent commitment to peace and justice, George looks to three pivotal events:

In Pulaski, in 1958, George attended his first clergy conference. His Bishop, John Vander Horst, called together the newcomer priests of the diocese. In the midst of the racial turmoil in the South, the Bishop gave an admonition: "I do not want you men to destroy the Church over civil rights." George had been buried in the stacks of England's Cambridge library for the past year, and before that in the other Cambridge library stateside. He hadn't given much thought to the role of the Church and civil rights. But his instinct was for the minority person, the outcast, the oppressed, the poor person sitting at the counter of the Regas Restaurant. The Bishop's invitation to timidity was the most effective advice since George Washington solicited the loyalty of Benedict Arnold.

In Nyack, George was greeted by a retired Episcopal priest who was a member of the Grace Church congregation. John Nevin Sayre was 75 years old, and George was 29 at the time. Sayre requested a meeting with the new Rector and asked him, "What's your position on peace?" "I'm for it!" George replied. "Well, what are you going to do about it?" The national headquarters of the Fellowship of Reconciliation, a peace organization of longstanding influence, was located in Nyack, and Sayre was a well-informed advocate. He never relented in his encouragement of George to pray and work for peace.

And finally, also in Nyack, George recalls the moment in August of 1963 when he wanted to go to the march on Washington led by Martin Luther King, Jr. But George had already agreed to be the camp director for junior high school students that week. The most he could do was read the news accounts of the historic event, and a column by James Reston on August 30, 1963, in the *New York Times* caught his attention. Reston wrote: "The first significant test of the Negro march on Washington will come in the churches and synagogues of the country this weekend.... And as moral principles preceded and inspired political principles in this country, as the church preceded the Congress, so there will have to be a moral revulsion to the humiliation of the Negro before there can be significant political relief."

George agreed, and he started a Wednesday night meeting to plot a course of action for the parish. He became chair of the Rockland County Conference on Religion and Race. The battle over these race issues in the church and in the community lasted for the remaining four years of George's ministry in Nyack. The idea of the Church as an outpost creating a moral ethos for social change became a key ingredient of George's work through the next three decades.

George remembers the low moments occurring in Nyack when epithets were hurled, the old guard of the church came to protest, and George was bruised but unbowed. He also remembers the high moments occurring when epithets were hurled, the old guard of the church came to protest, and George was bruised but unbowed. Agony and ecstasy flowed together. The church at Nyack became a center of peace and civil rights advocacy, and a place where people from the social margins of life were welcomed.

When Ken and Betty Rhodes flew to New York to interview George, and to share the desire of the parish of All Saints Church, Pasadena, for a continuation of John Burt's prophetic leadership, the match was apparent. George's sermon that weekend in Nyack was on interpreting the Lord's Prayer; his forum presentation was on the pros and cons of cremation. Ken and Betty admired the spirit and style of the young Rector. They were impressed that he could produce a forum schedule for a year in advance that included some topics even more exciting than cremation.

Ken and Betty flew home with a good impression and a good report. Ken's chairmanship of the Rector Search Committee would come to be regarded by him, and by many others, as a crowning life achievement.

"Take our hearts, and set them on fire, for Christ's sake."

The Sunday morning procession.

Chapter 6

Hearts on Fire

ON ANY GIVEN SUNDAY MORNING at All Saints, the scene reminds one of a carnival.

Music of many varieties floats through the air, from classical one might only hear in a church to rock one might never hear in a church.

People are flowing hither and yon—going to classes in the Parish House on the Bible or peace in the Middle East or the poetry of William Blake—or racing off to a meeting on the environment, wedged into a side room in between the main events.

Children are scurrying to the upstairs Learning Center and to Scott Hall and into and out of the Sanctuary for games and sharing and lessons.

Food is available at several booths—out of the main kitchen for the choir in between services, from a table where a mother-and-daughter team entice people to contribute a dollar to the food ministry for south central Los Angeles by offering them a "free" slice of cake, to a "Justice Bread" table where parishioners can buy baked goods made by the homeless of Los Angeles' Skid Row, to a catered brunch for the Women's Council in the Great Hall.

At the hub of all the programs and services is a quadrangle lawn overflowing with people hawking their wares from behind banners and tables with displays and literature. Write a letter to your Congress person over here, sign up for a small group experience, enroll your children in a summer camp, pick up some information on Central America, buy a handcraft from a developing nation, purchase a ticket to next week's organ concert, order a tape of the service and Rector's Forum over there.

Make a pledge and pick up your envelopes in the Stewardship Office. No need to wait until the fall.

Newcomers gather in the Rector's Office to make sense of all the activity, while a few others who have been coming for decades, and their parents before them, sit quietly in meditation in the Chapel, also trying to make sense of it all.

And in the big top Gothic structure to the south, the glorious services of worship—with a heterogeneous throng of people in the pews and 50 choir members coming down the aisle amidst crosses and candles and more banners held aloft by youth acolytes, trailed by a dozen vested clergy and lay readers, with prayer and scripture and anthems and sermon and eucharist and the kiss of peace, followed by an intimate interactive service of healing for a few who want to share their special needs with a priest.

Missing from the procession are the elephants and caged tigers. But apart from that, this could be mistaken for a carnival, with one significant difference: This is not about entertainment.

Sunday morning at All Saints is the nerve center for personal and societal transformation.

This outpouring of energy is presented weekly by people who have found meaning for their lives, and ideas they believe in, and who with evangelistic fervor invite others to participate. Transformation takes place because of the powerful interaction of sacred causes—local and global, in the family and in the community—with sacred quiet moments of forgiveness and inspiration.

Nothing is trivial and nothing is left to chance. Too much is at stake. The sound technician has checked the mikes and the custodian has monitored the air temperature in the church. The team captain has choreographed the acolytes. The altar is set with linen and silver chalices in strict conformity to a picture pinned to a bulletin board in the Sacristy. The anthem has been planned for a year and rehearsed for a month. The Rector has carefully crafted the sermon, spending one hour preparing for each of his 20 minutes in the pulpit.

This Sunday morning expression today flows from the first sermon preached by George Regas at All Saints on May 14, 1967. In that inaugural sermon George spoke about "The Church—Old Roots and New Vision."

The parish must be, he said, a fellowship in which people:
1. Meet Christ and have life changed and renewed.
2. Remain open and flexible.
3. Travel light.
4. Become aware of the world.
5. Create a launching pad for practical Christianity.

The sum of this charter statement would result over the next 28 years in creative liturgy, an expectation of personal transformation, an intellectual and theological search for truth, an engagement of contemporary issues, and a continuous series of experiments with the cultural implications of faith.

In the central arena of peace and justice, George set forth an array of challenges back in 1967:
1. Involving individuals in building a just order of society, a society which reflects the spirit of Christ;
2. Encouraging personal action in the continued crusade for human rights and the unflinching fight against every form of discrimination;
3. Going to work to lift the level of the community's life—

its housing, schools, hospitals, recreational facilities;

4. Being a peacemaker in a bitter and hostile world;

5. And finding an adequate and just way of taking the great wealth of this nation and providing a new and decent life for the poor.

One might correctly say that this manifesto both predicted and created the momentum that has pulsed through the life of the church and the broader community from 1967 until the present day. The parish responded with enthusiasm to this clear vision and to their new Rector.

The pages ahead will unpack the initiatives that have helped to carry out the ideas expressed in this first sermon. Not all of these ideas received the same attention as the years passed by. Doubtless the sermon, if it were written today, would have some different emphases. But by far the most amazing aspect of George's outline of a vision nearly three decades ago is the degree to which it has been implemented.

No one in the congregation that "opening day," including George Regas, envisioned a 28-year run. No one could have known the roller coaster of parish life that would careen through the ensuing years with some don't-lose-your-faith dips and some hold-onto-your-convictions highs. And the amount of nurturing education and pastoral care required to make the process work smoothly would be a monumental undertaking in itself.

The Rector has preached this inaugural sermon, refined and refocused, about 1000 times. He is guided by the advice that one should reshape an "I have a dream" speech about once each week. If your vision can't stand that much exposure, then perhaps it is not worthy.

Other components of the ministry of George Regas help make sense of all that follows. They are more implicit than explicit, but very powerful organizing precepts nonetheless.

George conceives his parish to be the community. No church can deal effectively with the complex issues of urban life without taking in the grand sweep of life in the neighborhood. When a new clergy person of whatever denomination comes to town, George is often the first to invite the pastor to lunch. All Saints is located right across the street from Pasadena's City Hall, and a well-worn path ties together the two centers of power. The people who make All Saints' community programs work are the most resourceful and committed people who can be enlisted for the task, regardless of their affiliations. There is no sense saving only the Episcopalians in town, when their salvation depends in part on how well the Baptists and the Methodists are doing.

Risk is an important component of discipleship. People never adopt new ways of thinking and acting without trauma. Taking bold stands, no matter how well-considered, is dangerous. Generosity is going out on a limb. New paradigms for society and for self are disconcerting. Being forgiven is a perilous responsibility. The lay people and staff who are most enriched by their experience at All Saints are people who first of all accept risk as a bright side to life, and only then do they work on minimizing its reckless and suicidal dark side. And the most ominous risk that one must work to minimize is the risk of the status quo.

Competence is a spiritual value. No matter how noble the church's ideals, competence is the engine that gives these ideals their impact. A prophetic sermon can be interesting or entertaining. Whether or not it makes a difference is dependent less on the inspiration of the preacher and more on the competence of those who are charged with carrying out the "therefores." I once was told by a minister about the chair of his Christian education committee, who didn't believe in teaching. He had been the chair for many years, during which time he effectively thwarted most of the progressive ideas that others put forward. Had the minister ever thought about firing the chairman? No. Because nice churches never offend nice people. And these same nice churches are dying because people don't take them seriously any more. The consequent ethos of ineffectuality that is permitted to flourish is an affront to the true spirit of Christ. George Regas has taught us that "the organization and management of resources are holy endeavors."

So these precepts, along with the vision outlined in the sermon preached on May 14, 1967, are guidelines for understanding the worship and work of All Saints over the past three decades.

In the mid-1970s the Bishop of Los Angeles, Robert Rusack, came for his annual visit to the parish. I sat next to him during the service so that I could carry out my assignment of assisting the Bishop throughout the morning worship.

Before his sermon George issued the call to hear the word of God with the following words:

> "Help us, O God, to be masters of ourselves, that we may become the servants of others. Take our lips and speak through them; take our minds and think through them; and take our hearts and set them on fire, for Christ's sake. Amen."

During the quiet moment after George's recitation of this mantra, under the watchful stained glass eye of Mrs. Myers hovering above the high altar, the Bishop leaned over to me and whispered, "Does he always say that?"

The Bishop had only been to the parish a few times, and I had only been in attendance for a couple years, but long enough to respond, "Yes, Bishop, I believe he does."

The other invitation that has become legendary at All

Saints during the Regas era is this: "Whoever you are, wherever you are on your journey of faith, you are welcome at the Lord's table." The invitation to the eucharist, the primitive rite of the Lord's Supper which means "thanksgiving," from "wherever you are on your journey of faith" is an altar call with a difference. It is decidedly not a traditional invitation out of a certain darkness into an absolute faith.

"Wherever you are on your journey of faith" is language that includes people of any religion or no religion, children and adults, people from many different ethnic and racial and creedal backgrounds, stalwart members of the parish and newcomers.

People who come to All Saints are not presumed to have lost their way any more than we have all lost our way. Each life is precious, and the place on the journey where we find ourselves can be a sacred place. Parishioners come from many different denominations, from many different theological and political persuasions. The congregation encompasses the richest and the poorest people in the community. On any given Sunday, without any apparent relationship to wealth or poverty, some are aglow with triumphant faith and some are almost visibly holding together the pieces of their lives.

The journey has no predictable destination, other than God. There is no minimum entry requirement of orthodoxy or respectability for participants. Some don't care for this kind of ambivalence, but many others are energized by the authenticity. The only clear understanding is that this is a transforming journey of the people of God, and if you have even the vaguest sense of wanting to be with this people, and with this God, then come.

The invitation also bears within it the acknowledgement that we all have our lives to offer. However impure, even at the moment of response, however in need of forgiveness and healing, however confused, this remains a very substantial offering. We are already on a journey that honors who we are—our diverse histories and experiences. For the sake of the community of other faithful people, we bring who we are with us for the next step in our faith adventure.

This eucharist does not obliterate who we are, because within our wretchedness there is the beginning of faith and the heartbeat of a new parish. The journey is both individual and corporate. The transformation is personal and social. The moment is intimate and public.

"Take. Eat and drink. This is the body of Christ, broken for you. This is the blood of Christ, poured out for you."

In my imagination, as this ritual is repeated each week, I see the people of All Saints taking the power of the eucharist into the world, and lifting the brokenness of the world into the healing presence of Christ.

The power of this ancient moment, when it invades our contemporary lives, is a stunning power. When a church lives out of this resource and bears witness to a surrounding community, year after year, the result is overwhelming.

Not every moment will be glorious, of course, as we shall see, but the invitation is worthy of our response, from wherever we are on the journey.

Chapter 7

The Jury Is In

THE QUEST FOR PEACE has been a main focus of the ministry of George Regas since his earliest days in Pulaski, Tennessee. But there, having rejected the advice of his Bishop to keep the church aloof from the struggles for civil rights that might consume it, George was just beginning his priesthood. He was not nearly as confident or authoritative on social issues, and the world was enjoying a post-Korea, pre-Vietnam respite. So George talked about the issues at his first parish, but the people of Pulaski largely were disengaged and George made little effort during his few years there to mobilize them in any controversial direction.

At Nyack he met with his conscience on peace issues, John Nevin Sayre, and much more ferment took place both within George and within the parish. George thrust himself with ferocity into the peace movement in his congregation and within the ecumenical community. Some became upset with his preaching and activism, and communist labels were applied, but radical conflict stayed mostly within the bounds of civility. While the struggle seemed epic at the time, the tempest in Nyack was only a dress rehearsal for events in Pasadena.

George, along with the rest of the country, was undergoing a growing ambivalence about Vietnam.

The national soul-searching was brought home with an

event that cast a pall over parish life in Pasadena. Jim and Harriet Fullerton had been pivotal to the success of John Burt's ministry. They were prominent in the business and social community of Los Angeles, admired for their integrity and for their conservative values.

Their son Jim had volunteered to fight in Vietnam, along with so many others, at the height of his promise as an educated, personable and upwardly mobile young American. He struggled to balance his idealism and patriotism with a growing experience of the reality of the war. He never returned from a long-range reconnaissance mission in March of 1969.

The Fullertons were at home preparing to go to All Saints on the fateful Sunday morning when the news arrived. The phone rang, but there was no voice at the other end of the line, then a few minutes later...a knock on the door by a U.S. Army infantry captain in full uniform. Not much needed to be said.

Two years later, when George was preparing for his own watershed sermon on Vietnam, there was never a doubt that the Fullertons would be consulted. The sermon was not at stake, but the life of the parish was at stake. George didn't need a committee to write his sermons any more than his predecessor did when he was talking about race relations. But what was being contemplated was not merely a one-shot catharsis on the morality of the war.

George, in close collaboration with his associate, Bill Rankin, was planning for a mobilization of the parish against the war.

Bill had been a curate at an Episcopal church in Elmira, New York, and a candidate for the Benny Goodman Orchestra, when George met him in New York City and invited him to join his new All Saints staff in the fall of 1967. Bill (who now serves as Dean of the Episcopal Divinity School in Cambridge) came on as youth minister and served until 1974, but his role quickly became much broader than just ministering to the youth of the parish.

As a result of a study conducted in the first year of George's tenure about the needs of the children of Pasadena, All Saints had begun a Foothill Free Clinic in 1968. Young people within the parish family and in the larger community needed access to psychological and medical services with regard to drugs, sexually-transmitted diseases, and other issues affecting young people. Since Bill was responsible for youth work, and since George considered the community as his parish, one can see the logical merging of youth ministry and social outreach and community involvement.

So the transition to having Bill ready to assume the direction of a Peace Operations Center to mobilize against the Vietnam War was not as much of a stretch as one might think. What could be a more crucial component of youth work than keeping the young people of at least five countries from being used as combat fodder?

One of the activities that laid some of the foundation for the bold initiative that George was preparing was the creation of a "Rock Mass" on one Sunday evening a month. The church was packed with teenagers. Busloads of youth groups were brought in to hear their contemporary music and share in an informal eucharist.

A few parents were alarmed. One stewardship caller was confronted by an older parishioner who had wandered into a Rock Mass only to be assaulted by the loud music and offended by the demeanor of youths seemingly hanging from the rafters. The parishioner increased her pledge with the comment: "George must be doing something right!"

There was a flavor of protest to these gatherings. Some of the music was anti-war. Some of the preaching reflected the anguish over current events.

But most of the energy and intelligence that went into his historic sermon of March 7, 1971, came from George's own pursuit of the truth about Vietnam. President Nixon had addressed the nation at a televised press conference on March 4. The war had been extended into Laos and Cambodia by South Vietnamese troops and American air power. The President had asked the further indulgence of the people "while the jury is still out" on the morality and winnability of the war effort.

George Regas' thunderous response was "Mr. President, The Jury Is In." He called on the parish to mobilize its resources to end the war.

Jim Fullerton had spent a week considering George's request for support. He stayed up until 4 a.m. Sunday morning on March 7, preparing his own remarks. He spoke from the lectern about his and Harriet's personal tragedy...and about their advocacy for George's position.

Bill Rankin announced a meeting every Sunday night for the duration of the war for those committed to peacemaking. This Peace Operations Center would gather people from throughout Pasadena and Los Angeles. It would educate and protest and lobby to end the Vietnam conflict. Prayer vigils and letter-writing campaigns became regular occurrences. The prophetic course of parish life was clear; the hard work of implementation was set in motion.

Even with the groundswell of moral outrage that George was able to tap, given the fact that the nation as a whole and All Saints in particular were registering their opposition to American policy, a contingent of parishioners still was incensed that their church would take such a position. A "Save All Saints" group was quickly formed, with some prominent parish and community leadership. The next Rector's Forum and the next Vestry meeting were devoted to the dialogue, which grew increasingly impolite.

George's sermon was reprinted in the *Los Angeles Times*. The firestorm of opposition grew. George lost his honorary membership in the Annandale Country Club, but not before he and Bill Rankin met the leaders of their opposition for lunch there. Rankin was called a Communist, and then the conversation turned nasty.

One of the couples in the church, William and Clara Burgess, was representative of the opposition. They were neighbors at various times and social friends of both Ken and Betty Rhodes, who used their tennis court, and of Jim and Harriet Fullerton. They still look back on George's position as traitorous, and Bill Burgess responded in a 1971 newscast interview and in a *Los Angeles Times* article, and said as much. Prior to the irreparable fallout with All Saints, Clara Burgess had worked with Bill Rankin to establish a home for children recovering from drug abuse.

But plenty of respectability and strength gathered around the peace mobilization side of the argument. People who were part of the business establishment applauded the courage of All Saints' position. As always on such cutting edge issues, some members of the parish wondered why George had taken so long to espouse publicly their stance.

Some social friendships were sacrificed; some members were lost. Bill Rodiger, an attorney who was George's confidant in the matter and Senior Warden at the time, counseled him to turn over to the "Save All Saints" group a roster of church members and addresses, even though they were lobbying for the withdrawal of pledges and the ouster of the Rector. Their meetings were announced without prejudice in the weekly parish bulletin. "It's their church too," Bill advised.

Bill Rodiger saw his job as one of keeping the church

together while being supportive of George's bold initiative. Over the next few months, George and Bill visited the homes of 100 parishioners—to listen, to share, to heal and to strengthen the work and witness of the church.

As a compromise measure to placate some of the opposition, Bill suggested to George that the financial administration of the Peace Operations Center be separated from the church, so that people who pledged to All Saints could at least say, if they cared to, that their money was not going for a cause they found detestable. But George vetoed the idea. He wanted the church, and not just the Rector under cover of the freedom of the pulpit, to be against the war.

In the end "Save All Saints" withered in its opposition. One member shouted at a meeting that he was withdrawing his pledge; Gene Burton whispered quietly, "I'll match whatever it is." The loss in members and money turned out to be not so very great, although the trauma was immeasurable.

Under the auspices of the Peace Operations Center, groups of the most unlikely people went to Washington, D.C., to sit in and to visit Congressional representatives. Sue Dragge was one of the most respected women of the parish and of the community. She had graduated from a prestigious Connecticut boarding school. She had contributed $12,000 to start the Foothill Free Clinic. She was a former head of the Flower Committee of the Altar Guild. Yet in response to the call to be a peacemaker she became one among many parishioners to be arrested in the Capitol Rotunda and to spend a night in jail. A search of the penal records of the District of Columbia reveals that Sue was the first former member of an Altar Guild to be incarcerated. Nice and proper and generous discipleship had matured into taking risks and exercising political courage.

George travelled with Leonard Beerman, the Founding

Rabbi of Leo Baeck Temple in West Los Angeles, and a newfound friend and collaborator on social causes, to Paris to meet with six delegations at the Paris peace talks. Clergy and Laity Concerned sponsored the foray, much to the consternation of America's political leaders. George received a gift book to commemorate the visit, with the inscription on the dedication page, "Blessed are the peacemakers, for they shall see Paris!" Leonard recalls with amusement George's disarming self-introduction to William Porter, the U.S. Ambassador to France, prior to their presentation of their concerns for peace: "I'm just a country preacher, but...."

The controversy had put All Saints on the national map, and from then on as issues arose there was more of an expectation of engagement. The unrepentant old guard would drift away from the church, with a bang or a whimper. A few who felt robbed of their parish would wait for George to be elected a bishop or to retire, so that they could reclaim their Anglican religious heritage.

George had declared in his sermon: "My hope is to radicalize the establishment—myself being one of them—and take middle America and give their good will and their desire to build a world of peace clearer focus and more effective power." This statement constituted his clearest offense. One almost expects the religious powers to be cautious about war and inclined toward peace. One can politely write off the embarrassment of church people meddling in international and military affairs. But don't ever go after the heart of middle America; don't try to convert those in power to your moral position. Don't treat the community as your parish, and risk the survival of your ministry on a position that could just as easily be a meek reminder of the Church's timid presence at the margins of life.

The Peace Operations Center continued its work until

1974, when Bill Rankin left to pursue his graduate studies in North Carolina. How successful it was can be argued endlessly, but the fact is that the nation continued to move in the direction of peace in Vietnam, and the moral judgment against the war is now a matter of historic record.

But Bill Rankin takes satisfaction from the notion that outward success is not the only measure, although it is important, of a congregation and its moral purpose. Faithfulness for its own sake is also a worthy goal. "It was not as important to demonstrate that we had changed the country, but that the country had not changed us."

Chapter 8

Making All Saints Famous

ONE OF THE PEOPLE attracted to All Saints by the Peace Operations Center was a young Catholic woman aspiring to be a nun and living at the nearby Mayfield School. Her name was Alice Callaghan.

Alice and her colleagues in the Order of the Holy Child Jesus were supportive of many of the same issues that found a home at All Saints. In particular, their support for the farmworkers and Cesar Chavez was a strong mutual concern.

John Burt had been a faithful ally of the farmworkers and a personal friend of Cesar Chavez and Chris Hartmire, who later headed the National Farmworker Ministry. Some of All Saints' parishioners, as mentioned earlier, were in the agricultural business. While the church eventually lost the participation of some of these members, others like Jack Wallace remained intensely loyal. Their devotion to the church was sufficient to transform their lives and transcend narrower economic self-interest.

Even J. G. Boswell, reputedly the world's largest grower, was a friend to the farmworkers up to a point. He donated thousands of dollars to the California Migrant Ministry in its efforts to improve the lot of his workers, largely Hispanic fieldhands who were brought across the border legally under the bracero program. This bracero program was designed to assure a labor supply to California farmers. But little was done to protect worker rights. The need for Chavez and the Farmworkers' Union was evident.

George Regas picked up where John Burt had left off. He visited Chavez in Fresno in the midst of a strike and witnessed the imprisonment of some church supporters of the union.

When the Migrant Ministry people, whose work was originally sponsored by the National Council of Churches, became supportive of the union and opposed to the bracero concept, Boswell and others withdrew their contributions. They resisted the inroads that Chavez was making with some of California's religious and political leadership.

Chavez and Hartmire had been to All Saints on several occasions. But George went one step further and invited Cesar to speak from the pulpit during the regular worship service. George and John before him were usually careful to have outside "provocateurs" hold forth at a Sunday Forum. The pulpit ploy was so intrusive in the eyes of some parishioners that a few walked out, and the next Sunday many voiced their protests to their new Rector at a specially-arranged dialogue session. George now feels that he made a tactical error in giving over the pulpit, but the damage was done.

In order to mend some fences George dispatched Bill Rankin to Phoenix at Mr. Boswell's invitation, and in his corporate jet, no less. Bill was to go on a fact-finding trip to view the working conditions at one of Boswell's Arizona ranches. Some common ground for future negotiation might have been possible, because Boswell at least in some ways had the interests of his workers at heart, hence his earlier charitable donations.

But charity is one thing, and political power is quite another. The whole adventure misfired because Bill didn't stick to the planned itinerary. He wandered into the fields and spoke with some of the workers in an unrehearsed setting. Boswell accused him of tampering and organizing the workers against him, at Boswell's expense. The possibility for accommodation evaporated in Arizona's desert heat.

The farmworker link and the opposition to the Vietnam War aroused enough curiosity in Alice Callaghan that she had to visit this church to explore. She wandered into a Rock Mass and liked the spirit of the place.

George tells the story, probably slightly embellished, of his first encounter with Alice. She explained who she was, and he directed her a few blocks west to St. Andrew's Catholic Parish. But in reality All Saints was and is a very inclusive place, and George is not in the habit of restoring people to their original denominational allegiance. (And Alice didn't wind up in the habit either, eventually becoming an Episcopal priest.) When Alice's commitment and skills became more evident, she began to work alongside Bill Rankin at the Peace Operations Center, and George hired her as a member of his staff.

As if George couldn't get into enough controversy of his own making, Alice began to lead the way.

She had an affinity for the Catholic Worker tradition, and had a lot of friends at the Los Angeles Worker community, where a "blood strike" was underway. The Workers took exception to the fact that hospitals had blood collection centers in the heart of Skid Row, preying upon people who didn't necessarily have good blood to donate but who needed the $5 payment. They tended to donate too often and without proper safeguards. The Catholic Workers had found incidents of blood contamination, and danger to both the donors of the blood and to the ultimate consumers.

Alice investigated the situation in Pasadena. She armed herself with some data and tried to get the attention of the community's two major hospitals, the Huntington Memorial Hospital and St. Luke. They initially took no action in response to her proposals.

Alice merely wanted the hospitals to contract with the American Red Cross instead of the less reputable Skid Row outlets. She proposed that hospitals run their own banks so that they could monitor the collection process and eliminate the abuses. She wanted hospitals to employ stronger disclosure methods for informed consent for blood users.

You might ask, "What does a Roman Catholic woman, preparing to become a nun, working at an Episcopal church, know about blood? This woman is obviously confused. Shouldn't her concerns be left to the experts?" This was the response of the hospitals at the time.

Of course, Alice had her own experts, who had been quickened in their conscience by her moral perspective. Dr. David Blankenhorn, an All Saints' parishioner, was a prominent physician whose expertise was crucial to the respectability of the cause. Alice bided her time for about a year, collecting information, consulting with the All Saints' Vestry, and waiting for the hospitals to do the right thing.

When it came time to play some public relations hard ball, Alice had the support of George and the Vestry. A press conference was held in George's office, and two of Pasadena's most reputable institutions got a little bloodied in the exchange.

They were swift to repent, and each opened its own blood bank, with the safeguards Alice knew they would have to take if their own personnel were in charge. They in turn prevailed upon All Saints to conduct periodic blood drives under the auspices of the American Red Cross. And they agreed to stricter informed consent procedures.

The word "confrontation" is not usually found in the vocabulary of Christians. It was near the top of the vocabulary list of Mara Moser, however. And the work described above—with the farmworkers and the Peace Operations Center and the hospitals—could not have issued in a good result without a willingness to confront evil. Such confrontation has a biblical base in the approach of the Hebrew prophets, the ministry of Jesus, and the practice of the New Testament church.

But confrontation involves risk of embarrassment or defeat. It calls for doing one's homework and making a stand based on competence and expertise, rather than on rhetoric and moral fervor alone. And the issues outlined above would not be relevant to the church's work unless the whole community were viewed as the parish.

One of the discoveries in the unfolding activism of All Saints is the obvious need for "champions." Either laypeople or staff people must push a concern, whether it is for children's education or for empowering the poor, in order for the status quo in any of these areas to change. The Kingdom of God, in other words, doesn't just happen on its own. People have to identify their values, do their homework, rally their support, and persevere in their cause.

One of the gifts of George Regas is a kind of converse leadership. When a concerned lay person presents a cause that the church simply must address, that person often concludes the pitch with the question, "What are you going to do about it?" Or, as Mara Moser asked John Burt, "What's the matter with your church?"

But George is apt to reply, "What are you going to do about it? What's the matter with your church?"

In more recent All Saints' history, Steve and Charyl Padgett came to All Saints in the early 1990s. They were a young couple with a burden for the proper stewardship of the environment. Even a cause this compelling doesn't flourish on its own merits. Steve and Charyl put the issue to George, and George gave them his blessing but very little of his creative energy. A Rector can only be creative in so many arenas at one time.

The emergence of EDEN!—Environmental Defense of the Earth Now!—is an example of a program that is far better because grassroots lay leadership created it. Steve and Charyl's tragic death in an automobile accident caused the mantle of leadership to pass to Jennie Bevington—the "Queen of Eden"—and her husband, Eric Seyfarth. And now the torch is being passed again. The competence of Steve and Charyl's contribution has enabled EDEN! to flourish in their absence.

COLORS—Christians Offering Love to Overcome Racism in Society—is another example of the excellence of lay ministry, of people who adopt a cause, who become its champion, and who make All Saints famous because of their promotional zeal. In the aftermath of the Rodney King beating and the Los Angeles uprising, a few lay people called for a gathering of African-American parishioners. A surprising group of 100 people showed up, including blacks, Asian and Hispanic members, along with 20 whites. The agenda was open-ended, but in part it focused on the lack of diversity on the church staff and the apathy of the congregation, a bit too smug in its assertion of liberality in race relations. This group was not only lay led, but to some extent staff-confrontive. Today their efforts include a constructive ongoing dialogue, complemented by consciousness-raising educational offerings and awareness workshops and historical exhibits.

George's most important contribution is not being the champion of every good cause. But the atmosphere at All Saints is one in which champions are encouraged to come forward. They don't have to be belligerent about it, but they have discovered that an aggressive posture helps. And this is an atmosphere that George has deliberately created. The skills of lay leadership are elicited. And they must push and pull the rest of us into compliance with their vision.

I recall a staff meeting at an all-day retreat we have a couple of times a year to consider overriding ministry initiatives. There were about a dozen of us in the room, and we each had ten minutes to make our case for our priorities for the coming year. I was in the early years of my leadership of a ministry called Union Station, an outreach to homeless and hungry people in Pasadena that was begun by All Saints and Alice Callaghan.

An advertisement had been appearing on television with regularity about an upstart casino operator in Las Vegas named Steve Wynn. He owned the Golden Nugget Hotel. He concluded his television commercial with the brash assertion: "I'm going to make Las Vegas famous!"

Of course, Las Vegas already was famous. There wasn't much that he could do to add or detract from its reputation.

When my turn came to talk about my dreams for Union Station, I uttered my well-rehearsed line: "I'm going to make All Saints famous!" And everyone snickered at me as I knew they would.

Somehow the aura that has been created for us around the staff table is the expectation that we have a unique and wonderful contribution to make to the life of the parish. So today Jim Walker has a vision for the music and liturgy; Kristin Neily has a vision for the senior high youth; Barbara Jones has a vision for the smooth operation of parish life; and Javier Benitez has a vision for the maintenance of our physical plant. The vision and the competence to implement it are the standard expectation.

George Regas surrounds himself with staff and lay leadership who want to make All Saints famous. (Why do you think I'm writing this book!?) Famous for its liturgy and for the gloss on the parquet floors. Famous for the way we reach out to those who are homebound or to the newcomer. Famous for our conduct of a wedding ceremony or a funeral.

And we make no apology for this level of expectation. Sometimes staff and lay people get their feelings hurt because they are held to a standard that they think should only apply to people in the arts or business or athletic competition. All of the good ones in these disciplines are trying to become famous, by the way.

It was written of Jesus that his fame spread throughout the land. We are, along with Jesus, also dealing with the ideas and values of the Kingdom of God. A touch of bravado and a healthy ego have their places in the work of All Saints Church. If we didn't have some measure of each, we would probably not rise to the substantial challenges that our parish and our community present to us.

Chapter 9

The Gospel Sting

A CHRISTMAS EVE SERVICE at All Saints is a powerful moment.

About 50 parishioners and what seems like a similar number of custodians and an Altar Guild contingent have worked for a day to polish the pews so that a rich scent fills the air, to deck the halls with evergreen and magnolia, and to set the altar for the Christmas eucharist. At Christmas Eve, the music and the liturgy will be gorgeous. The proclamation of the gospel from the center aisle and from the pulpit will stir the soul. Everything is ready.

And then, into the magic of this holy night, the people come. Some in furs and some in sandals. Some who are new to All Saints and one or two like Ken and Betty Rhodes and Adele Barnes. All of them bring their histories with them. The money they put into the plate for the Christmas offering represents their lives, of course. But as I look out over the expectant throng I see the substance of a year's worth or a lifetime's worth of offerings of conviction and devotion. If I spot Edna and Ernest Banks and Lydia Wilkins in the crowd, my Christmas is complete. There are many champions here tonight. This night represents a gathering together of the faithful, in all their brokenness and wholeness, with all their gratitude for a relationship with God and their yearning for forgiveness, with their memories and their hopes. Some have lost their way during the past year, and some have found it.

And when the flourish and the substance of these precious lives seem to be in balance with the flourish and the substance of the pregnant moment, the procession begins. The birth of the Christ Child is the gift of God that invades this moment and infuses our own lives with dignity, meaning, fame and immortality.

People at All Saints have discovered this secret that the substance of life is their devotion to Christ. They thrive on this reality, even when they don't have the words to define it, even when they are inarticulate about their faith. Sometimes their actions are obscure. They visit an elderly parishioner in a nursing home. They comfort a person who is dying from AIDS. They are working at 1 a.m. Sunday morning to set up the chairs and tables for the myriad gatherings that will occur in a few hours. They work in the office behind the scenes to support the work of an incredibly productive management staff. No one notices or takes their picture. There is not usually a press conference or a sermon to highlight the meaning of their devotion.

But they are making All Saints famous, nonetheless. And deep in their bones, they know it.

People at their best don't just create paintings or run companies or play baseball. People—even those working on the assembly line—want to make their mark. They really want to make a difference. Deep down within, and transcending almost every other human yearning, they want to be immortal.

The church, more than any other institution, has the opportunity to bestow immortality on people. For us the issue is not whimsical, like hitting the ball out of the park or making a million dollars selling widgets. Even the heroes who perform those feats, which are so ephemeral, think they're changing the world. They are trying to become so famous that they make their way into the Hall of Fame.

But in the Church, we are following a leader and a 2000-year-old tradition that says, "Love never ends." When we leave behind our bigger barns some day, what we have done in the name of love will stand forever. We really are changing the world! We are laying up treasure in heaven, which is the New Testament equivalent of the Hall of Fame.

Our rallying cry is that we are "making all things new." We are recreating the world here and now according to the values of the Kingdom of God. This is heady stuff. Filled with a sense of unparalleled opportunity and the risk that goes with it, we take up the challenge.

If we can do this without an ounce of bravado, then wonderful. But a bravado-free environment is not the goal of All Saints Church. Some people are more flourish than substance, which we can tolerate to a point. Some people are more substance than flourish, which we love, because we can provide the flourish more easily than the other.

Armed with a profound understanding of human nature, coupled with the resources of God, the Rector has a powerful weapon. When you are dispensing immortality, you can pretty much have your way.

On the surface, the "gospel sting," All Saints style, is to have lunch with a parishioner and ask for a chunk of his life, or several thousand dollars of her portfolio. When the Rector invites you to lunch, you had better beware. The Rector has spent 28 years setting the table for this engagement.

When the Foothill Free Clinic was founded in 1968, Sue Dragge wrote out a check for $12,000 for the first year's rent of a vacant doctor's office, over lunch with Bill Rankin and the Rector. Jim Cockburn got off easy. His wife Martha came home from a planning meeting for the new Union Station, in 1973, and Jim anted up $1,200 for a year's rent of a small storefront.

I recall the day in 1985 when we invited Bob Yarnall to a meal at the old Huntington Hotel in Pasadena. Bob possessed some accounting and computer skills that we sorely needed to make our Union Station ministry run more efficiently. Anne Wycoff was the chair of my Union Station Board, I was the executive director, and George Regas was the Rector of All Saints Church. We all had our roles to play, and we had rehearsed our parts.

We knew Bob Yarnall was about to retire from ARCO, because we kept in touch with our parishioners enough to know what was going on in their lives. Bob Yarnall was no ordinary parishioner. None of them are. But Bob was a past member of the Vestry whose style was very conservative from a fiscal and political point of view. His integrity was above reproach, and he was very helpful in keeping the excitement of the expansive vision grounded in reality.

When the Vestry was sorting out its position on Nicaragua, at the height of the political controversy over the role of the United States in that country's life, Bob became part of a 1984 fact-finding mission. The United States had blocked the application of Nicaragua to the World Bank. It seems the Nicaraguans were engaged in gunrunning. Bob, Jane Olson, and Millie Moser visited the U.S. Embassy to view the evidence. It consisted of a picture of a man rowing across a bay from Nicaragua to El Salvador with four rifles. Bob returned from Nicaragua a changed person, and because of his reputation and unquestioned patriotism, the Vestry had little trouble in endorsing a policy in opposition to our country's support of the Contras and attempt to destabilize the Sandinista government.

(Jane Olson's daughter, Kristin, later went to work for the World Bank and in 1992-93 she oversaw the allocation of $250 million in loans for Nicaragua.)

But let us return to the Huntington to understand the dynamic of this mealtime conversation. Its importance is not so much in the fact that Bob wound up being a nearly full-time volunteer accountant for Union Station in his retirement years, although that was a tremendous boon to our ministry. The significance is in the dynamic of what might be called the "gospel sting."

The reader may remember the 1973 Oscar-winning movie called *The Sting* with Robert Redford and Paul Newman. They carefully orchestrated the scenario so that their "mark" would bet and lose $500,000 in a foolproof scam. The mark was Robert Shaw, and they catered to his appetites for revenge and reward in such a way that he walked right into their trap. (In a deeper way that the movie didn't develop, his primitive appetite was to be a mark in the first place.)

The "gospel sting" is a variation on this theme without all of the tawdry manipulative elements, just a few. On our side of the table, we had the supreme bargaining chip—meaningful involvement, immortality. Bob Yarnall, our mark, had the remaining years of his life to give away as a Union Station volunteer. He wanted to be appreciated. The poor guy didn't have a chance. He made some noise about considering our offer—his life for...well...for nothing that he could exactly understand, nothing tangible. He went home to think about whether he could afford the time and aggravation to be Union Station's bookkeeper, while George and Anne and I broke into a little celebration that was not premature, and the pianist at the Huntington played a Scott Joplin ragtime piece.

When Bob Yarnall died a few years later, after giving much more to Union Station than even we had envisioned, after bringing us into the modern era in terms of our books and other administrative matters, our priest Clarke Oler spoke at his memorial service. "Bob liked his career at ARCO," Clarke said, "but he loved his work at Union Station!"

The key to a successful gospel sting is the understanding that you are not taking anything away from people that they don't want to give you. In fact, they will be liberated by the transaction. People are immortalized not by what you give to them, but by what you ask of them.

This is even, if not especially, true of the poor, who are oblivious to being offered something but seldom have the wonderful experience of being asked to make meaningful use of their lives. Jesus freed and healed more people with questions than with answers. You must have that deep appreciation of another person's gifts. You have to believe that your work is the most worthy and serious work that could possibly engage you and the person sitting across from you. Tell them that you need them. Tell them how critically important their contribution would be. Tell them what the vision is for your ministry together.

The variety of sting operations at All Saints, inspired by our Rector, is innumerable. The Rector has been known to ask for a million dollars over dinner, with the other person picking up the tab. Some of us on the staff have become adept at the sting in our own right. The procedure is not meant to deprecate the commitment of the laity, or to make us out to be manipulative. George's example to us is filled with grace and integrity.

And if the process comes with authenticity, and with the leading of the spirit, then the chances for success are great. Of course the risk of rejection is ever present, along with the risk of offending someone with your audacity. "How dare you ask me for a million dollars!"

Yet most of the time, even when the answer is "No," the people are flattered that you think so highly of them. You have honored them with your request.

A large part of George Regas' success with the gospel sting

grows out of his morning time with God and with the blank slate. The spirit brings to his attention those from the parish and from the larger community who are waiting to be asked to participate.

Jane Olson is an All Saints' parishioner who received an ominous luncheon invitation to meet with George Regas, Rabbi Leonard Beerman, and Harold Willens. These three had been casting about for a way to implement their concern to reverse the international arms race, which was not only threatening the survival of civilization but was robbing society of the resources to meet human needs for food, housing, education and health care. They had a vision, but it was at this stage undefined. They had come up with the idea of a major conference on "Reversing the Arms Race." Later in the planning process the theme poster would be developed with the slogan: "End the Race or End the Race."

Jane is a bright and wonderful person who could have had a more carefree life, had she not met George Regas. Husband Ron is a partner in one of the premier law firms in the United States. Jane was substantially involved in contributing her time and creativity to the arts and education. Her mornings with the *Los Angeles Times* used to begin with the feature and lifestyle sections.

Today she turns first to the pages of opinion and international news. "I would rather be going to Azerbaijan than Tahiti," she now says.

And she does go to Azerbaijan, as a member of the board of Human Rights Watch. She has been to more world trouble spots than Henry Kissinger.

George knew with some divine instinct that Jane had the potential to make a difference with her life. So the Regas-Beerman-Willens threesome invited her over lunch at the Beverly Hills Tennis Club to plan and direct a conference, a task that would consume the better part of a year.

Jane laughs today when she recalls her initial response: "What's the arms race?"

George had the prophetic insight, born of the Holy Spirit, to see in Jane a woman with vast untapped resources. He was able to elicit from her more energy and creativity than even she knew that she possessed. For the sting to work, all the parties involved have to embrace a faith that some capacity for a new challenge lies beneath the surface.

All Saints Church made a man of great faith out of Bob Morton, who began with the question, "Do I have to believe in God?" And we nurtured in Jane Olson a woman who has had an immense impact for the good of humanity on international affairs, beginning with the question, "What's the arms race?"

The people who know most about the arms race are often the least likely to reverse it. Knowledge can become a barrier to liberation. And the people who know most about God, in Jesus' day and in our own, are sometimes the least likely to be champions for God's Kingdom.

Early ecumenical leaders of the Interfaith Center to Reverse the Arms Race: The Rev. George Regas, Archbishop Roger Mahony (now Cardinal Mahony), Jane Olson, Rabbi Leonard Beerman.

Chapter 10

The Peace Journey

AN ARSON FIRE DESTROYED the historic structure of the All Saints Parish House in the spring of 1976, leaving only the Gothic stone shell. The Sanctuary and an adjacent office building had been spared. But the loss of space for classrooms and meetings, for youth education and adult forums, was a catastrophic loss. The extensive libraries of David Farr, the organist and choirmaster, and of George Regas had been consumed.

The parish was first traumatized, and then energized by the staggering calamity. The Parish House had been a center of power and transformation in the life of the church.

By the fall of 1979, three years of design, fundraising and construction had come to fruition, under the lay leadership of Bob Egelston and the staff leadership of George Regas and Doug Vest, coupled with a multitude of parish worker bees and donors. The new facility would greatly enhance the life of the congregation. And in part to honor those who had contributed a total of $4.5 million, and to carry out the mission of the church, the meeting and conference space would be put to good use by groups inside the parish and by the community at large. A facility ought to be used to facilitate.

Any evening of the week you can visit All Saints Church and find collections of people you may have never seen before, carrying out purposes that are compatible with the church's wider vision, but without the church's direct sponsorship. This is consistent with the goal of the rebuilding program, and with the notion of the whole community as the parish.

In the spring of 1979, at the time Jane Olson went to her luncheon, All Saints was making plans to rededicate its Parish House. George thought that the first use of the magnificent new building ought to be of the greatest significance. And the most significant stirring in his conscience was the need for the world to take seriously its suicidal plunge into nuclear disaster—the arms race. Would there be a way to use the new All Saints facility to gather faithful people to address this most critical issue?

The Peace Operations Center had closed down a few years earlier, and the war in Vietnam had ended. A group called the All Saints Peace Committee had been active beginning in September of 1978, under the direction of Dick Gillett, the priest who took the place of Bill Rankin, and a lay woman named Dorothy Kilian.

So there was a lot of precedent in 1979 in the parish for another mobilization against the powers and the principalities. This time the focus would not be on a particular war, but on the cold war in general. Peace is more than simply a political position, as important as that is; it is also a lifestyle orientation, with political implications. Peace is a lifetime journey.

Dorothy Kilian had come to All Saints with her husband Henry to join the Peace Operations Center in 1971. They had worked hard for international understanding at a neighboring church, where Dorothy was the bulletin editor and always got in her two-cents' worth for her causes. In 1970 George Regas had written her a note, even though he had never met her, that read "I love you for what you do for peace." Dorothy was surprised that someone outside her congregation at the time would read her bulletin and respond.

Shortly after they came to the Peace Operations Center, Henry died of a heart attack at the age of 58. Dorothy was adrift. She had to decide whether to give up, or work for peace in memory of her husband. Now over two decades later, her choice has become clear.

Dorothy made the transition to All Saints as a member after she attended a Rock Mass. "If I ever was born again, it was at a Rock Mass," she recalls. If this is true, she is in the church record books as the oldest person ever to be reborn at these youth-oriented services.

In addition to the Center, Dorothy became active in a program called WH/EAT—World Hunger/Effective Action Together. Dick Gillett, the new Director of Parish Program, had preached his inaugural sermon in the fall of 1974, and it was followed by a six-week course to consider the "therefores" of the sermon material. The nation at the time was in touch with the threat of world and domestic hunger, and thanks to the oil crisis the notion of scarcity had begun to infiltrate the psyche of comfortable America. Some of Dick's remedies for the crisis had to do with reconsidering lifestyle choices.

Lifestyle issues have always been difficult for All Saints to engage. It is one thing to protest a far-off war, even though it involves the loss of friendships and the social stigma of being a peacenik. It is another to decide to live more simply and to connect that decision somehow with compassion for others and the preservation of the planet. These were the concerns that WH/EAT (and now to a great extent EDEN!) had on its agenda.

Dick's sermon had another effect, besides bringing scores of parishioners out to study the issues. One of the conservative members of the Vestry suggested to George Regas that he fire his new associate.

Prior to his hiring, Dick had confessed to George that his

previous assignment as a priest in Puerto Rico for three years had led him to become a socialist sympathizer. (Where is the John Birch Society when you need them?) Dick had founded the Puerto Rico Industrial Mission as a bridge among labor and business and government interests, and as an advocate of environmental causes. Two American copper companies, in which the national Episcopal Church held some stock, were dumping their toxic waste in Puerto Rico. Dick got the church hierarchy to study the issue and disinvest, which brought Presiding Bishop John Hines so much criticism from some of his capitalist colleagues that he later summarized his involvement in the affair with the words: "It was a painful privilege!"

But George believed in having a lively and diverse staff. Not everyone had to preach the same sermon. George appreciated Dick's candor, and felt that the interplay of ideas on social issues could benefit from his constructive participation. So George respectfully but firmly told the Vestry member, "If he goes, I go."

Anne Blankenhorn, wife of Dr. David Blankenhorn, became the lay leader of WH/EAT. They formed a Food Co-op so that parishioners had an option of healthier and more responsible foods at cheaper prices. They sponsored a Soup Night once a week, with families giving up their normal more elaborate meal, shifting the savings to their Soup Night can to benefit world and local hunger ministries, and expressing their solidarity for those billions of people around the globe for whom a meal of soup is a great treat.

Dorothy Kilian and Barbara Bair designed a "Household Resource Audit" for each parish household, so that we could all be more responsible about our consumption of meat, energy and water, for example. But this was not just a denominational issue, so the audit forms were also taken to Sacramento and presented to a State Senate Select Committee.

WH/EAT organized itself around three committees, each of which had its champion. One committee was concerned for lifestyle, one for local hunger, and one for systemic issues. To advance the cause on all these fronts, Anne began to publish a WH/EAT Newsletter, which became a valued source of material to assist in lobbying government, changing personal habits, and learning about the global complexities. The newsletter was mailed out for many years to people in 20 states, as well as to members of the parish.

Some of the stalwart members of WH/EAT had a moral commitment to peace in Central America. Militarism was counterproductive to feeding hungry children. A little group of them formed a contingent called Women of Conscience, with Alice Callaghan leading them in some protests of United States' policy toward refugees. These were very proper ladies, very much establishment types in many outward respects (with the exception of Alice). But in their hearts they were radicals.

One of their most memorable exploits was a protest in front of a refugee detention center located on Fair Oaks Avenue in Pasadena. They filled a rented truck with mannequins that they had dressed and smeared with a red dye to simulate blood, and then dumped in the driveway of the center. Some of us will never forget the preparatory scene on the quadrangle lawn at All Saints one afternoon, with women of the parish scurrying about and bodies in various states of preparation spread all over. The body count represented the number of El Salvadorans killed in one day because of the military support of the United States.

Everything went according to plan, complete with extensive media coverage that Alice had orchestrated, until Javier Benitez, our Supervisor of Custodial Services, drove the truck to the public dump when the protest was over. One of the bodies fell onto the freeway en route!

A Central America Ministries committee was born out of the tragedies relating to U.S. involvement in those countries. The committee is still active in working with refugees in Los Angeles, in visiting Central America to support humanitarian development, in promoting peace, and in educating the parish and the general public. All Saints declared itself to be a "sanctuary" church and began to offer assistance through its members to Central American refugee families.

Grace Hall and Mary Parmenter are two longtime participants in the effort. They are most active in helping refugees to find jobs and food and shelter once they have come to the Pasadena area. On one occasion, in an attempt to unite a Guatemalan family, Grace and Mary found themselves helping two teenage boys to escape the life-threatening oppression of military conscription in their native land.

Grace and Mary had flown to Mexico City to arrange the necessary linkages for the trip north for the teenagers. After the transportation and border crossing arrangements were made, the All Saints duo returned to the United States to wait for events to unfold. At the appointed time, Grace and Mary checked into a motel in San Ysidro, just north of the border, with $600 of their own cash to pay the last installment to the "coyote." They were told to leave the lights off and wait for a knock on the motel room door.

Once the boys were in Grace and Mary's custody, the last leg of the trip to Los Angeles would be undertaken. Grace would fly with the teenagers from San Diego, and Mary would drive by herself to outwit the immigration officers stationed at the checkpoint on Interstate 5. She would proceed directly to Los Angeles International Airport to await Grace's arrival.

Unfortunately, Immigration and Naturalization Service representatives also check airplanes periodically. Two agents boarded the plane in San Diego, with Grace and the boys nervously watching their movement down the aisle. What to do?

Grace was 74 years old at the time. She didn't fit the INS profile of a smuggler. She went into her doddering old lady routine, and accidentally emptied the contents of her oversized purse in front of the approaching agents. They spent the next few crucial minutes rounding up cosmetics rather than Guatemalans. And by then the plane was ready to take off and confrontation was temporarily avoided. The agents happened to be flying to Los Angeles, however, so Grace had to carry out another ruse upon arrival at LAX. But even INS officials can be diverted by means of a compliment.

"You men were so wonderful back there in assisting a helpless old lady like me," Grace expounded. "Could you tell me the name of your supervisor so I could write him about what a credit you are to your profession?" The Guatemalan teenagers slipped down the ramp while the agents were handing Grace their business cards. George and Mario, the two boys, would be reunited with their families and proceed to complete their high school education and attend Pasadena City College.

Compassion does not respect artificially-created international borders. The quest for peace depends upon working against violence, and working at the same time to meet the legitimate needs of human beings, regardless of national origin. God is first of all the protector of the stranger and the alien. This is one of the central messages of the Hebrew scriptures, and one of the chief reasons that Jesus got in trouble with the political and religious leaders of his day.

On another international peacemaking front, Jane Olson, as a member of the Vestry, had become involved in the consideration of a Vestry endorsement for the Nestle boycott. Nestle was aggressively marketing a baby formula in developing countries, discouraging breast feeding by the new mothers. There was an international outcry and a call for a boycott of all Nestle products until the parent company redirected its promotional materials. WH/EAT was, of course, a leader in the fight. But the Vestry takes its oversight role seriously. They require information and homework from the staff and lay leadership, and they appointed a small group in 1977 to make a recommendation. The homework was so thorough that the Vestry voted for the boycott.

Having succeeded in completing this assignment, Jane was ready for bigger challenges. Or at least George had come to that conclusion in the privacy of his daily contemplation.

Harold Willens was appointed by President Jimmy Carter to be a delegate to the United Nations Special Session on Disarmament in 1979. George invited him to speak at a Sunday morning Rector's Forum early that year. He was impressed by Willens' plea that the religious community had to become involved in the moral consideration of the arms race. The Pentagon was an institution of immense power, which had to be brought into dialogue and accountability by people of faith.

George revived his contact with his esteemed colleague, Rabbi Leonard Beerman. Beerman and Willens were longtime friends. "How do we answer Willens' challenge?" George wanted to know.

All these questions and programs flowing together brought to the fore the idea of a conference, inviting the religious community to engage the morality of the arms race. Labor leaders, scientists, economists, psychologists, government and military officials, and clergy would be invited for a weekend of interaction with the members of Leo Baeck Temple and All Saints Church.

In April of 1979, with about a half year to plan this huge logistical undertaking, Jane Olson was summoned. Apart from not knowing what the arms race was, Jane was the perfect choice.

The conference exceeded the expectations of its planners. A total of 1200 people participated, spending Friday evening at the Temple and all day Saturday at All Saints, a great inaugural use of the new Parish House. The information communicated was so compelling, and the enthusiasm so palpable, that the leaders gathered for lunch on Saturday with a supreme question: "Where do we go from here?"

Leonard, Harold, George and Jane made the decision over lunch to announce the formation of the Interfaith Center to Reverse the Arms Race. Jane agreed to serve for a few months as the first executive director. The Center would be located in the Parish House, and the ambitious goal would be to end the cold war and the mindless accumulation of military weaponry.

Lay leadership of unparalleled commitment rose to the challenge that the Interfaith Center presented. Anne Sutherland, a reporter for the *Pasadena Star-News*, had covered the conference for her newspaper. She became a convert, so much so that she would change careers to become, first, Jane Olson's successor as executive director of the Interfaith Center, and, second, an Episcopal priest. Rick Thyne and Tony Wolfe and Linda Moore from the ranks of the Presbyterians assumed key roles. Parish laypeople such as Rick Felton and Katherine Littlewood carried the work when the baton was passed to them. Judy Felton became especially active along with Dorothy Kilian and Marty Coleman in leading groups of parishioners on trips to the Soviet Union. Marty, a Presbyterian laywoman struggling to define her faith in the context of public policy, became director of outreach for the Interfaith Center and is today a full-time lay member of the staff at All Saints.

These empowered lay people adopted an issue that had been placed upon their consciences by George Regas, and its demands aroused within them a surprising quality of leadership, exercised in a variety of interrelated ways.

Information was gathered and brochures were printed. Other conferences were planned and held. The most intense effort centered on the formation in every possible church and temple of a group whose purpose would be to mobilize the grassroots citizenry to expose the cold war as a facade created by governments to divert the people of their countries from the pursuit of peace.

At All Saints, as one among many of the member churches of the Center, the original Peace Committee took the name Critical Mass and continues to be active (now under the name of Peace Journey) in protesting and educating and lobbying with regard to the issue of nuclear arms. Among other activities, they sponsor Desert Witness sojourns to the Nevada testing sites to conduct prayer vigils and civil disobedience. Some members choose to subject themselves to arrest for trespass. Friends of the USSR and US/Soviet Relations groups, under newer names, carry out people exchanges and educational and cultural programs to help break down barriers that have been erected since the close of World War II.

After a ten-year run, the Interfaith Center closed its doors in 1989. A celebration dinner officially brought down the curtain on this chapter in the peace witness of the parish. There was and is still work to be done. But the end of the cold war was a milestone that offered a substantial victory, at the same time that it made the potential for fundraising to support the work much more difficult.

A more recent witness of the parish was in opposition to the Persian Gulf War. The highest moment in this brief but devastating conflict was a gathering of 1,300 people in Los

Angeles at the Islamic Center. Leaders from three faiths—Leonard Beerman, Hassan Hathout, and George Regas—called for people of conscience to reject the universal dependence upon brutal force, and the lies upon which such use of force has been based at least in Vietnam, Iraq, and Kuwait.

George has always worked hard at being open to people from other faiths. The legacy of cooperation among Jewish and Islamic and Christian leaders is a milestone contribution of his career.

The quest for peace took a fresh turn when three young black children were gunned down on the streets of Pasadena on Halloween night, 1993. A shock wave swept through the community. We knew about gang activity in our neighborhoods and an occasional drive-by shooting. But this senselessness mobilized many religious and civic leaders. At about the same time, Jack Scott, president of Pasadena City College, and his wife Lacreta, both members of All Saints, suffered the loss of their son to an accidental gun blast inflicted by a friend showing off a weapon.

George Regas asked Jack Scott to join him in a meeting with the Chief of Police and City Council members and many other interested parties to plan a response. The result was an ongoing effort at reconciliation called the Coalition for a Non-Violent City. We had learned something about reversing the international arms race. Now we had to consider how we could create alternative after-school activities for youth and limit the flow of weapons and ammunition in our own city. George's leadership skills in convening and coordinating a host of citizens and agencies came to the fore. A year after the deaths of the three boys, a citywide conference of 800 people led to a strategic community plan to change the environment of violence in all its forms.

The struggle for peace has many dimensions and never ends.

Leslie Learned, Rector of All Saints Church from 1908 to 1936.

John Frank Scott, Rector of All Saints Church from 1936 to 1957.

John Harris Burt, Rector of All Saints Church from 1957 to 1967.

George Frank Regas, Rector of All Saints Church from 1967 to 1995.

Greetings on the lawn following the Sunday worship, circa 1970.

Devastation of the Parish House fire in May of 1976.

Final worship service in the old wooden church at 132 N. Euclid, which served the congregation from 1889 to 1923.

The renovated sanctuary, 1991.

A September picnic on the lawn following a "Homecoming" worship service.

The AIDS Posada candlelight gathering of 7,000 people in the street between All Saints Church and Pasadena's City Hall.

Two questions need to be raised about all these parish and interfaith activities in the pursuit of peace.

First, do they make a difference? Does Mikhail Gorbachev, for example, even remember the occasion when Marty Coleman visited Moscow and gave him a "huggable planet"? Marty had pinned a picture of her granddaughter Amanda to the globe before presenting it to Gorbachev, who is also a grandparent. They talked about their grandchildren with tears in their eyes, and about forming a group of "Grandparents for Peace."

Dorothy Kilian's response is this: "People tell me I've made a difference, but I don't know. I can't imagine living any other way, in any case. To follow Christ is what I want to do. It makes me feel good, keeps me from vegetating, and gives me a sense of gratification."

Jane Olson asserts that violence is born of fear. The opposite of love is fear. Much of the answer, therefore, is in meeting people and knowing people. She now works on refugee and human rights issues. She knows children who live on the other side of the world. "If we don't trust in the goodness of God's plan and in the place of love in the universe, then we tend to hold onto everything that supports our exclusive notion of who we are, and we shut ourselves off from the dignity of others who are also God's children."

Jane continues, "There is more spiritual belief in refugee camps than I imagined. God is present among the survivors. They've taught me about faith and generosity, rather than vice versa."

So Jane copes with this new world that she's discovered in the last 15 years by maintaining her belief in the basic goodness of people. She is empowered by doing something rather than nothing, although she is not under the illusion that she is changing the world.

If I were Dorothy or Jane, I would be personally taking

credit for the collapse of the Berlin Wall. In reality, we don't know exactly how those epic sea change events take place. Political power changes hands. Economic equations are rewritten. Public opinion shifts. The Spirit of God moves. Perhaps all of the above occur in some unpredictable dynamic of cause and effect.

In the process, we become "prisoners of hope," much like our friend Desmond Tutu. The belief in individual and social transformation becomes a given rather than a titillating option. We must change the course of our civilization when it comes to violence. We must change our own lives. This is what our Rector has taught us through his own commitment and imagination.

The second question is much easier to answer. Is all this activity, mostly educational and political in nature, linked in any way to spiritual formation?

Listening to Dorothy and Jane speak provides a wealth of inspiration and biblical and theological insight. They represent hundreds of All Saints parishioners, many of them their colleagues in the peace movement, who have discovered Christ in very powerful ways in their lives. If "God is in the work" in any fashion, God is surely in the work of peace.

After returning from a recent trip to Cuba and another to Bosnia, Jane came to church and wept throughout the service, the way you weep when you come into the presence of God.

Union Station welcoming the homeless to its earliest Union Street location.

Chapter 11

Rich and Poor Together

IN ADDITION TO BEING across the street from City Hall, All Saints is only five blocks east of the intersection of Fair Oaks Avenue and Colorado Boulevard, the heart of Old Pasadena. Today this area is a trendy upscale entertainment and shopping center, but in the 1970s it was home to about a dozen second story hotels filled with the elderly, disabled, mentally ill and alcoholic. Many more of these folks roamed the alleyways or made a home for themselves at either Central Park or Memorial Park.

Alice Callaghan called together a small group of parishioners in 1972 to explore ways the church could reach what she presumed to be a needy population on our doorstep. This group and others in the parish knew that part of the journey of peace has to do with meeting the needs of the poor.

The first task was to find out the real needs, rather than have an establishment church impose its own programs on an unsuspecting populace. So Alice visited the hotels and bars to meet the clientele. She reported back to her committee on the possibility of opening a storefront where people could come to sit and visit, to have a cup of coffee and play a game of cards. People could go to the park and the nearby library, but they had no other wholesome places for socialization or activity.

In preparation for the church's plunge into Old Pasadena,

All Saints sponsored a neighborhood dinner in Central Park on Christmas Day of 1972. Alice had run off some flyers and posted them around the neighborhood and left batches in the hotels and bars. People from the church brought turkeys and hams and casseroles. The group that showed up from the church had a wonderful Christmas and so did the people who came for the holiday feast.

Next the committee had to find a site, and when one was finally located on Union Street, just west of Fair Oaks, Jim Cockburn came forward to pay the rent. You can imagine what can be rented, even in 1973, for $100 a month, so the volunteers set to work to paint and provide card tables and books and chairs. The name Union Station was chosen because the committee wanted to avoid the condescension implied in the notion of "rescuing" the poor, or founding a "mission" to convert people to Jesus, as if the poor needed religion more than the parishioners did. Union Station had a nice positive ring to it. For the same reason of respect for personal dignity, the people who visited the Station were called "patrons" rather than clients.

Volunteers were enlisted and trained, two to a shift, five days a week, to open the doors and mingle with the guests and keep the coffee on. Someone brought in a crockpot for a little soup. About 20 people came each day to sit and visit and eat.

Soon people like Annabel Griggs and Adah Kunzelman, the Thursday afternoon crew, brought in a dozen hardboiled eggs each week for sandwiches. Each week, that is, for about 18 years! Jean Lewis is still going strong on Saturday mornings after 21 years. Alice must have had these folks sign long term contracts with no escape clauses. They were a hardy group of parishioners.

I was completing my master's degree in 1974 at Fuller Seminary, just a block over from All Saints. My wife Sybil and I were Presbyterians, but we had ventured over to All Saints to go to Rock Mass and because of our sympathy with the stance against the war. I had decided to sidestep the ordained ministry path and focus on working with the poor in a church setting, if possible. If that was the focus of the gospel and of the ministry of Jesus, it was good enough for me.

All Saints' Union Station was about the only game in town, so I got to know Alice and some of the volunteers, and when I completed my course work I talked to Alice about a job. I knew Union Station didn't have much of a budget, but Sybil and I had figured out that we could live on $300 a month during the one year that she would require to finish nursing school at Pasadena City College. My plan was to get a part-time job to earn the $300, and then spend two or three days a week being an on-site social worker for Union Station. The volunteers were wonderful, but they only came in once a week and didn't have the time to help patrons with jobs or rehabilitation or housing.

Alice had an even better idea. "If you are willing to work for $300 a month, why don't I see if I can raise that money so that you can just work full time at what you really want to do?" So we decided to rendezvous in a week to give Alice time to raise the $3,600 required for the year.

I still don't know exactly what George and Alice cooked up, but I'm sure they set up a sting operation with someone, and I began my work in the fall of 1974.

The work grew as more people heard about our little hospitality center, and as we found more creative ways to befriend and assist our patrons. George didn't require me to join All Saints Church, but that became a natural choice as I grew more comfortable with the volunteers, almost all of whom in the early days were parishioners. I enjoyed the liturgy, the central role of the eucharist, and the outstanding preaching and music. When Sybil completed her degree, I had come to like my work so much that we decided to stay at All Saints, especially when I was offered a living wage.

In 1976 the Parsons Corporation came to Pasadena and the City's Redevelopment Agency wanted us to find new quarters so that our block could be leveled to make way for a Parsons' parking lot. After months of searching, with the city's help, we found a central location on Colorado Boulevard, with twice the space. The rent was much higher, but we had developed some funding sources and were able to sign a two-year lease with a two-year option.

About this time some of the property owners had begun planning for a resurgence of commercial interest in Old Pasadena. The poor didn't have a part in their ideal scenario. In fact, the hope was that the hotels could be redeveloped as office space and the bars could give way to restaurants.

Our landlord had never heard of us during our two years on Union Street, just two blocks away from his retail store. Despite the use of the word "mission" in our lease, he thought we were a nice church with a reading room for senior citizens, he claims.

His business colleagues were shocked. "You did what?" they exclaimed in disbelief. So the next day when we arrived to begin fixing up our new site we discovered that our landlord had locked us out. I was meek and mild, being a seminarian and former Presbyterian of the "nice" church persuasion. But Alice was combative, and she wasn't about to allow the poor to be pushed out of their new home. She called up a lawyer friend from the church, Bob Carlson, and a good locksmith, and we met at the Colorado Boulevard site very early the next morning. We had the locks changed again, and when the landlord arrived at his shop next door he called the police to have us arrested for trespass. Bob Carlson showed them our lease, whereupon they explained to the landlord that this was a civil matter about which they could do nothing. We coexisted with our reluctant landlord for the next four years.

I went off to study social ethics at the University of Southern California during this time. But during my absence from the social work side of the Station, Alice made me chairman (volunteer) of her Union Station board and custodian (paid), to help me get through school. When I finished my course work, Alice went off to England at the suggestion of Bishop Rusack, to study for the Episcopal priesthood, and I became the new director of Union Station (and still custodian).

In 1979 I was working directly for George Regas, since the Station was still an outpost of All Saints Church. I met with him to explain that I really wanted to make the Station my career. We already had some volunteers from a few other churches. The WH/EAT group at All Saints was supplying some of our food budget. Our work was expanding. We could publish a newsletter and get the word out even more. Homelessness was becoming more of a front page issue in the United States. Couldn't we come up with a budget of, say, $30,000 a year if I promised to work at raising some of that from other groups? That was a momentous meeting for me because George's encouragement set Union Station on a path of unprecedented growth.

When it came time to find a new home, our landlord not being willing to extend a lease that he regretted giving to us in the first place, the pace of Old Pasadena revitalization made it impossible to relocate. All Saints had a small building just north of its parking lot on Euclid. We decided to move there temporarily in 1980. That building remained our home for nearly ten years.

One of our patrons, Dennis Pettigrew, had died on the

streets of Pasadena from exposure and hypothermia in 1983. We called together clergy and lay people from several downtown Pasadena churches to begin planning for a shelter component to our program. In March of 1984, a year after Dennis' death, we opened a 20-bed shelter in the basement of the nearby First Congregational Church, first under the direction of David Patterson and then of Cynthia Abbott.

During the decade of the 1980s we began a "Patio Painting Class" when Lee Hill volunteered her talents. We expanded our hours and upgraded our food so that we were serving two meals a day, six days a week. We developed a strong board of directors, including representatives from other congregations, and in 1985 we incorporated as a separate nonprofit corporation. Volunteers from everywhere came to us because we were telling our story to every willing group of two or more listeners all over town, and we were circulating our newsletter to thousands. We were adding interns and part-time staff from among Fuller Seminary's students to provide friendship and counseling to our patrons. We began a health screening project and a literacy class. Bob Yarnall joined us as our volunteer bookkeeper and Ernest Banks continued his work as our volunteer food buyer. Frank Cook cleaned the Station every day, even though he complained regularly about the laggards among the poor, because it was his Christian duty. We hired Frank Clark to coordinate our volunteers and Diane Williams to plan our menus.

During this period an elderly couple in our parish called me up and asked if I could come over for an afternoon cup of tea. Murray and Marian McDougal were wonderfully resourceful supporters of Union Station, and I sensed a sting in reverse. They had something to give me.

Marian had just inherited an unexpected $18,000 from Olivia Young, her late housekeeper, of all persons. The

McDougals had no need of $18,000, but they thought I might be able to use it in some special way at the Station. We were in the process of planning a new effort to provide recovery services to our patrons who were addicted to drugs or alcohol. The money would enable us to hire a professional, himself a recovering addict, named Bill Morgan. Bill's philosophy is, "We ask people to do things they've never done before in order to become someone they've never been before." This philosophy coupled with the power of the Twelve Steps has transformed the lives of hundreds of our patrons.

And all of these programs in the 1980s took place out of our "temporary" quarters adjacent to the church with a kitchen the size of a walk-in closet.

But a prior event would change the future of Union Station dramatically, and this also had to do with the serendipitous receipt of money.

Toward the end of 1982, we were struggling to make our budget, as usual. But our annual experience indicated that we would receive a few hundred dollars in checks dated December 31 as soon as we opened our New Years' mail, so our board was not particularly worried. When I eagerly came to the office on Tuesday, January 3, 1983, I opened a letter from Dorcas Davis in Ojai. She was a retired lady from West Virginia whom I had met only once or twice, but I knew of her interest in our work with the poor through a mutual friend. Inside the letter was a check for $10,000.

No one had ever given me a check for that amount before. Our board decided we couldn't show a surplus for the year, as that would send the wrong signal to the supporters we were cultivating on the basis of our desperate need. So we transferred the money into our newly-established "Building Fund."

We found a plot of ground about a half-mile south of

Colorado Boulevard, and out of the way, we thought, of Old Pasadena redevelopment interests. The Humane Society was up the block, and our site had been a former scrap metal collection yard. We thought we could use the location to recycle lives rather than metal and be humane to people in addition to animals. It cost us about $200,000 just for the land, but we had a new confidence that we could raise the money and build a permanent home on Raymond Avenue.

A wealthy woman who lived over a mile away from our site, and just across the street from George and Mary Regas, decided she didn't like the prospect of poor people being so close to her walled estate, with the crouched lion statues at her gate ready to pounce on intruders or passersby. She actually lived as close to the Euclid Avenue site as to the proposed Raymond Avenue site, and I doubt if a homeless person had been on her street in years. A few other business neighbors on Raymond Avenue had some legitimate concerns about our proposal for a 6,500-square-foot, two-story, hospitality center and shelter, and we eventually dealt with their concerns through some constructive negotiation and compromise. But they allowed themselves initially to be co-opted into the crusade of this wealthy woman, whose presence at our public hearings decked in furs and jewelry exuded arrogance. The newspapers got hold of this savory story, and people from all over town who had never heard of us before began to rally to our cause.

When we finally took our case for a conditional use permit to the Pasadena City Board of Directors, we had worked for several months to cultivate our support. On the evening of May 21, 1985, George Regas rose to address the Board:

"We have come here tonight to show our concern for the poor. Our city has a moral obligation to allow us to proceed. Not all of us can speak tonight," George acknowledged, "but I would like those who are here as advocates of the needs of the poor in our community to stand up to register their support."

About 1,000 people rose silently to their feet. People who lived in mansions and people who had no home stood shoulder to shoulder. When compassion gains a hearing in the secular political arena, and prevails, the thrill is an incomparable expression of the Kingdom of God on earth, as it is in heaven. The vote of the City Board was unanimous on behalf of Union Station. And many people look back on that evening as one of the most memorable events in the history of our city, and in their own journey of faith.

These 1,000 people were not standing for the Nicene Creed, of course. Nor did we celebrate the eucharist or take up an offering. This was a hearing before the City Board, not a church service.

But George Regas has taught many of us that these also are sacred moments. This is where the people of faith gather, if they are serious about changing the world and experiencing their own transformation.

We still had to deal with a lawsuit, which delayed the process for a couple more years. A very small group of disgruntled opponents took Union Station and the City of Pasadena to court to protest that we had not complied with the need for an environmental impact report. We had considered the potential blight of noise and traffic adequately, but we hadn't addressed the blight of poor people in and of themselves. Our opponents argued that the very presence of the poor, coming to our new facility for food and shelter and recovery, would constitute a negative environmental impact on the surrounding neighborhood. The stereotypical economic prejudice of their position was unbelievably insensitive to the humanity of millions of Americans. Judge John L. Cole of the Superior Court listened attentively to the novel argument; then he thundered from the bench, "Balderdash!"

Once again Union Station prevailed and we opened our $1.2 million facility in the fall of 1989, fully paid for with $225,000 in government grants, about $150,000 from foundations, and the rest from private sources. I have often told Dorcas Davis that her $10,000 check, which began our building fund, became the most highly leveraged contribution in the history of charitable giving.

Throughout Union Station's history, George had held up the idea that we had to work for systemic change, and not just address the crisis needs of the poor that Union Station was used to dealing with. Why are so many people poor, unemployed and addicted? Can we do anything in our society to prevent the polarization and alienation that we encounter each day at 412 South Raymond Avenue?

Toward the end of the 1980s, I informed my Union Station board that I wanted to spend more time developing affordable housing, which was not part of Union Station's initial agenda, but which was certainly continuous with the needs of our patrons. I resigned as director at the beginning of 1990.

Today our Union Station staff numbers 20, our volunteers over 400. About 50 people a night stay at our two shelter sites, and up to 225 a day eat our meals. More than 200 form a recovering group of alumni—the "Here We Grow" group. Three twelve-step meetings are held at the Station each day. Our budget is about $900,000 a year. Last Christmas, at our 22nd Annual Christmas Day Dinner-in-the-Park, more turkeys and hams showed up than there were people at our first dinner in 1973. We have also, for the past 21 years, sponsored a Central Park feast at Easter and Thanksgiving.

The story of Union Station has become so familiar to me that I am prone to underplay the spiritual dimension of this work. There is no cross above our doorway. We don't evangelize at the Station. But to me the site at 412 South Raymond

Avenue is the most sacred spot in Pasadena. This is where rich people and poor people come together to share life, and God is in the midst of the transaction.

We have always emphasized that we are not the helpers and the helpees. All of us at the Station are searching for meaning for our lives. We have much more in common with one another, but we have allowed society and its stereotypes about who poor people are and who rich people are to separate us into two camps.

Unfortunately, in Los Angeles in recent years the perception of two camps is a powerful and oppressive metaphor that defines much of our culture. In the midst of our recent urban unrest, All Saints has forged an alliance with the Praises of Zion Metropolitan Baptist Church in south central Los Angeles, and George Regas and their pastor, Joe Hardwick, have become great friends. Our congregations visit twice a year, we exchange preachers, our children go on weeklong retreats together. We have tried to break through the barriers that separate black and white and rich and poor.

One of the symbols of this eventual solidarity is captured in a simple story. Every year since 1973 a group at All Saints called Alsamigos gathers together Christmas gifts for our patrons at Union Station. One year a member of the group suggested that the gifts be personalized in a small way. So the wrapped presents to unknown homeless people would be marked as Orville Dill marked his package that year: "Large man's sweater, from your friend, Orville Dill."

Orville didn't personally know any of our patrons. But one day shortly after Christmas, a large man approached one of our Station volunteers. He was wearing a brightly colored sweater.

"That's a lovely sweater you have on," commented the volunteer.

"Yes, thank you. It's a Christmas gift from my friend, Orville

Dill." When this story was relayed to Orville, he couldn't get over the fact that he had actually made a difference in a poor person's life.

Just as the Berlin Wall fell, some day the artificial barrier between the rich and the poor will come down around the world, and we will make friends across the chasms that divide humanity into separate camps. People who are wealthy and people who receive only one gift at Christmas are yearning for and reaching out to one another.

Our crisis is an issue of statistics—the statistics of polarization. But it is also a matter of the spirit—the separation of brothers and sisters from each other and of children from their God. We must solve the economic issues at the same time that we solve the spiritual issues. We make the sandwiches and provide the shelter, as we chip away at our own fear and ignorance.

A feast for the poor sponsored by Union Station.

Chapter 12

Housing as a Cornerstone of Justice

WHAT CAN A CHURCH DO to combat the problem of homelessness in urban America?

Union Station as it now exists is much more than any one church can do. If we knew back in 1973 what opening a little storefront on Union Street would eventually entail, Jim Cockburn might never have given the $100 a month for the first year. We might have been intimidated by the challenge of raising $70,000 a month in the 20th year.

Those biblical proverbs about the "evil of the day is sufficient" and "give us this day our daily bread" are God's admonition that present faithfulness in response to the present challenge is all that we can expect of ourselves and of God's provision. Rent the storefront and pick up the day-old donuts at Winchell's and see what happens next.

Yet this approach is too piecemeal, unless it really is part of an open-ended search for opportunity. As we talked to our patrons in the early days, needs beyond the need to have a cup of coffee became apparent. People's lives unfolded before us, and we were still the people of faith with access to the resources of God. So in a thoughtful way we could be responsive.

The ten-year plan of a John Burt really does have a place if it is a statement that we understand faith to be incremental. Truth is revealed in stages. Obedience is bite-sized, but the underlying appetite is voracious. And the resources of God are beyond our present imagining. God owns the cattle on a thousand hills.

So what can a church do to combat the problem of homelessness? One thing…and everything. Don't be so traumatized by the problem that you fail to put your foot on the path toward a solution. And don't be so mindless that you try to solve a problem in a single day that it took you decades to create.

In one sense George had very little to do with Union Station. It wasn't his idea. Alice and a small group of parishioners were its champions. And George knew better than to micro-manage either the program of Union Station or the person of Alice Callaghan.

But George created the seedbed in which such ideas might take root, and the staff environment where people such as Alice might find a niche. The importance of creating an expectation of heroic action, and an atmosphere in which risk, and therefore failure, is acceptable, is obvious. The work of our staff today flows out of this same expectation.

When George Regas talked about openness and flexibility in his inaugural sermon in 1967, his second point, he might have been talking about the growth of Union Station. In fact, that entire sermon served as a blueprint for Union Station's evolution, even though neither Alice nor I was present.

1. Meet Christ and have life changed and renewed.
2. Remain open and flexible.
3. Travel light.
4. Become aware of the world.
5. Create a launching pad for practical Christianity.

Union Station itself became a launching pad for a new program created in response to a new opportunity. The old Young Men's Christian Association building in Pasadena's Civic Center was the last bastion of single-room-occupancy housing in the city. This SRO housing is the most affordable variety for many of the people who are among our patrons. They rent a room for a few hundred dollars a month, and share bathroom and kitchen facilities with others on their floor.

Business and political interests had succeeded in eliminating almost all Old Pasadena's SRO housing. At Union Station we had always complained about the dilapidated nature of this housing, because even though our patrons lived in hotels like the Star and the Ritz and the El Rey, the facilities didn't quite live up to their billing.

Across the nation economic and social policies have led to the near-elimination of SRO housing in our urban centers. The growth in homelessness has roughly corresponded to the prevalence of these policies.

So when the YMCA signalled its desire to get out of the housing business in Pasadena, Union Station was faced with the prospect of having about 150 more homeless people on our doorstep. Where else could they afford to live? No one was building new affordable housing for single adults to replace the old.

The Associate Rector at All Saints, Denis O'Pray, and our director of Operations at Union Station, Cynthia Abbott, began to work with the Y and the City of Pasadena to see what could be done. At the Station we had our hands full with our new facility. We couldn't afford to spend the energy or the money on a new project.

We were able to get the City to fund a study of what the closing of the Y would mean in terms of the homeless population. The study documented what we already knew, that the loss of SRO housing would continue a citywide trend and increase the numbers of people on the streets.

At a Union Station board meeting, we asked for an indication of interest from our member churches. Would they be interested in forming a new nonprofit for the express purpose of buying the YMCA, renovating its 143 rooms, and preserving the affordability of this housing? The next month three churches—All Saints, Pasadena Presbyterian, and St. Andrew's Catholic—indicated an interest. So two representatives from each of these congregations joined with two representatives from Union Station to form the Pasadena Housing Alliance, a new nonprofit corporation.

A few years later, with about $12 million in largely government funding, the Y was reborn as Centennial Place. It stands today as a glistening example of what concerned people can do when they dig in their heels and refuse to allow economic and social policies to bring about the disintegration of a neighborhood.

In the meantime, Alice Callaghan had returned to Los Angeles, now ordained, but the same basic Alice, to begin a program on Skid Row for Hispanic families, called *Las Familias del Pueblo*—the Families of the City. Most of her board came from her old friends at All Saints, who conveniently happened to be some of the leading capitalists in Southern California.

Alice's philosophy was to shape a vision that could be the vehicle for a desired social change, then find the people with the political and economic clout to get things done. Alice would more or less lock herself in a room with those people for an hour, at the end of which they would have her vision and she would have their power.

The vision in the mid-1980s was to buy up all of the run-down hotels on Skid Row—about 65 hotels in a 50-square-block area—renovate them with the help of federal and state tax credit money from corporate investors and the Community Redevelopment Agency of Los Angeles, and put them into the ownership hands of nonprofit housing corporations. The nonprofits would provide social services to the residents and keep the rents affordable.

The first three hotels to be purchased were the Roma, the Pershing and the Pennsylvania, and the first nonprofit sponsor was the Church and Temple Housing Corporation. All Saints and Leo Baeck Temple had a collegial relationship going back to George and Leonard Beerman's Vietnam War activism. The relationship had been solidified through the Interfaith Center to Reverse the Arms Race. Now these groups were brought together again to go into the Skid Row hotel business.

Alice called me up to see if I wanted to sign on with her new adventure. Her call coincided with my desire to withdraw more from my Union Station responsibilities, and to tackle the systemic causes of poverty, so I went to Skid Row to live at the Roma, initially, then at the Pershing, and finally at the Pennsylvania, which my new Church and Temple board had renamed the Genesis. We had plans to accompany Alice on a journey through the books of the Bible, since the number of books roughly corresponded to the number of hotels she wanted to buy and renovate.

The experiment was wonderful while it lasted. Members of the two congregations came down in small groups to paint rooms, to have potlucks with the residents and to take them on recreational outings, to meet with our Resident Council to plan activities, and to conduct AA meetings. We hired a social worker named Ulric Van den Berghe to come to the hotels two days a week to meet with residents and prepare a noontime meal.

Steve Moses of the Temple, whom many of us thought to be a direct descendant of the great Hebrew liberator, chaired our board, and Russ Kully from All Saints was the co-chair.

Russ also supplied his law firm office a few blocks from Fifth and Main, where the hotels were located, for our monthly board meetings.

We had a great concern to be equitable in the relations between the two congregations, and the two faiths. We used to joke that both Leo Baeck and All Saints could claim the preeminent position in the naming of our group—the "Church and Temple Housing Corporation." As far as we were concerned, the church was listed first. As far as the Jews were concerned, the temple was in first position, since Hebrew is read "backwards." This good cheer permeated the relationships of the members of our joint board.

Sandy Ragins had succeeded Leonard Beerman as the Rabbi at Leo Baeck. One of the most meaningful moments of my life was when I stood next to Sandy at a combination Christmas-Hanukkah party at the Genesis. (They thought it was a Hanukkah-Christmas party.) He was singing with reverential gusto, "O Little Town of Bethlehem."

Sandy had told us of the Hebrew tradition of the people of Yahweh being menders—"tikkun." The "tikkun olam" were the "menders of the world." Sandy told me I was part of that tradition, and I counted it a privilege.

Somehow this was life and faith as it was meant to be. We were discovering truth. We were creating a more just society. Our lives were being transformed.

And then in the early 1990s the whole experiment failed with regard to Church and Temple's role. The hotels are still there, though the potential for social service enrichment has not been realized. But it became obvious that our interests and the needs of the Skid Row Housing Trust, the nonprofit which Alice had created to oversee the hotel process, were not compatible.

When you just want to be a nice church, everything is compatible. When you are driven to accomplish a goal, niceness sometimes gets in the way.

At key points along the way my own inadequacies were apparent. I had a Master of Divinity degree, not a degree in hotel management. I was trying to balance what should have been a full-time job in Los Angeles with my continued work with Union Station and directly with All Saints. A series of management companies failed us. The Skid Row environment was incredibly hostile. Prostitutes and drug dealers and muggers paraded up and down our street with impunity. The finances of the project never worked for us. Some of our residents were more than we could handle.

There is not much sense in talking about a great urban church and its accomplishments without acknowledging the risks and the real possibilities for failure. The Church and Temple board still exists, now looking for another housing opportunity. And I personally wonder whether I will ever again get to stand next to Sandy Ragins singing Christmas carols.

Ulric Van den Berghe now works in the much tamer atmosphere of Pasadena, but he is still overwhelmed by the numbers of people who come for assistance and by the stories their lives represent. What a challenge he undertakes each day, with an unflagging dignity and spirit of compassion. When Union Station moved from its site at the north end of All Saints to its permanent location, the church had to reconfigure its response to the street people who continued to come to its doorstep. Now it wasn't quite as simple to refer them up the block. Every urban church has a growing share of drop-ins, especially a church with the size and reputation of All Saints. So when we discontinued Ulric's work at the hotels we increased his presence at the church to four days a week, where he meets the needs for friendship and support of a host of needy people, including a few he first met on Skid Row.

I have refocused my own commitment to affordable housing. The work of places like Union Station, providing emergency services and rehabilitation to hundreds of patrons each year, is short-circuited unless society can allow for recovering people and the working poor to have access to decent housing.

So at All Saints we have formed two corporations, one called Affordable Housing Services, a nonprofit, and one called Keystone Housing Enterprises, a for-profit.

Keystone is a product of collaboration between All Saints and the La Canada Presbyterian Church, which also has an ownership stake. The nine individual owners of Keystone are members of one of the two churches or of the community at large.

The Keystone vision is to bring our capitalist friends back into the affordable housing arena, not as do-gooders but as investors. All the charity in the world, and all the government programs, will not meet the projected need for seven million additional units of affordable housing within the next decade in urban America. So the engine of capitalism, which is so efficient and productive when it comes to many of its more trivial pursuits, must take upon itself the moral pursuit of providing housing for the poor. Keystone believes that such housing can not only be provided, but that in many cases it can generate a decent return on capital to those who invest.

And Affordable Housing Services also has much work to do. It shares with Keystone the same vision, but has additional access to charitable and government funds to fulfill the vision. It is charged with making sure that residents of affordable housing have access to social services that can enhance their lives and enrich their spirits.

All Saints has also participated in programs like Habitat for

Humanity, building home ownership opportunities for poor people around the world and in Southern California. Some of our members have invested on their own initiative in sober living centers for those who are in recovery from alcohol or drug abuse. Some have invested in Madison House to provide housing and support for Central American refugees.

Providing housing to the poor, with enlightened ownership and humane management, is a good investment in the future of our cities. In fact, the absence of housing is creating an urban abyss of unprecedented proportions in America. Ask anyone who has been to the corner of Fifth and Main or to the MacArthur Park area just west of downtown Los Angeles recently how they feel about the future of our country.

Affordable housing is not a panacea. The swirl of social issues is almost irretrievably complex. But housing is a good place to begin to unravel the urban crisis. It is the "keystone" in the arch of all the other resources that must be made available if the United States is to succeed politically, economically, and morally in the twenty-first century.

George and Mary Regas with All Saints' Centennial Banner.

Chapter 13

Keepers of the Vision

ON THE EVE OF WORLD WAR I in London, Sir Edward Grey looked out on the city. Darkness had fallen, and people were safely indoors for the night.

Working late and fearing the gloom of war, Sir Edward saw the lamplighter making his rounds to extinguish the street lights, which had served their earlier evening purpose. He commented, "The lights are going out all over Europe, and we shall not see them lit again in our lifetime."

As poverty, addiction, unemployment, hunger and homelessness descend upon the cities of the world, we might share the same feelings. We are coming to the close of a century that has been undeniably the most brutal in the history of civilization. Adrift on a sea without a moral anchor or an intentional destination, our generation is searching for some structure and meaning for the unprecedented progress and prosperity that also, ironically, mark our existence.

One of the metaphors that might be used to capture the spirit of All Saints Church is the metaphor of lighting the lamps once again in our cities. Through the evolution of this urban church, we attempt to bring hope back into the life of our community. Few people personify this activity more than John and Denise Wood—two deeply spiritual people, very elegant in bearing, calm in demeanor, and committed intensely to the betterment of their world.

Denise had no church upbringing; John's father was an Episcopal priest. Their religious inclinations did not coalesce around a church, therefore, but initially around a movement called Moral Rearmament. Moral Rearmament had been founded in the aftermath of World War I to elicit the best from people—friends and enemies alike—toward the creation of a new social order without war. The Holy Spirit, in a very non-sectarian sense, is the source and convener of the latent goodness in people. The potential for a humane society is greater than the potential for destruction.

While Denise was majoring in chemistry at Vassar, just prior to World War II, the Moral Rearmament movement became her spiritual home. She learned to listen to God, and she learned that spiritual concepts and the people infused by them could make a difference in the world.

When Denise retired as Dean of Students at the Marlborough School in Los Angeles, she presented herself to her parish ready to put herself into service for these beliefs.

John had already made his mark at All Saints. He served on the Social Concerns committee of the Vestry, which had decided to focus on unemployment in Pasadena. John volunteered to explore the situation.

One of the obvious needs was for the creation of a training center where residents who were out of work or underemployed could acquire new skills. The idea had been floated twice before by city officials, without success. No one was able to coordinate the various community groups whose interaction would be required to make such a skills center happen.

But John was wonderful at bringing people together—a good listener and mediator with an absolute trustworthiness and no apparent ego needs. Every church could use a few people like John.

In 1979 John became the chair of a task force with representatives from All Saints, the City of Pasadena, Pasadena Unified School District, and Pasadena City College. Meetings were held once or twice a week in the newly rebuilt Parish House over the course of many months. A tremendous momentum and spirit of cooperation developed, resulting in the creation of the Community Skills Center, the first of its kind in California. The Center opened its doors in September of 1980, with 1200 students, mostly post-high school, enrolled in a large variety of practical courses. John was asked to lead the Community Skills Center board.

John tackled another issue on behalf of All Saints while he was serving as the Junior Warden in 1980. The Pasadena Redevelopment Agency was pursuing ambitious building plans for the Los Robles Avenue corridor. Some neighborhoods were not having opportunity for input and were being underserved by the process. The church had some interest directly because our own property was adjacent to some of the Los Robles sites. But as John chaired the church's task force, he made it clear that the first priority would be advocacy for the interests of the poor. The Vestry accepted the recommendations of John's committee, and John and George Regas appeared at a City Board meeting to call for a slower pace and more community involvement. The City agreed to moderate the flow of development and make the process more democratic.

In the early 1980s, under the auspices of All Saints' Centennial Planning Committee chaired by Lou Fleming, the parish had decided to make a "Gift to the City." Don Miller, a layman, came up with the notion that Denise Wood's newly available time could be harnessed by having her visit leaders from every area of city life and listen to their perceptions of urban need and opportunity. George Regas asked Denise if the church could hire her for three months to go out into the community—the larger parish—just to listen. The shape of what would emerge from these interviews was not known, but the process itself would be worthwhile.

Denise met with and listened to 104 people. She calls this endeavor "grazing"—going about with no aggressive agenda simply to glean information. She met every Thursday morning with Denis O'Pray, Lou Fleming and Don Miller to share her findings and receive direction on whom to see next.

Listening can be a very powerful spiritual discipline, and very much a part of the transforming power of the Holy Spirit in the life of an individual and a community. George Regas had discovered that in his study. Denise was putting her Moral Rearmament background to work in the offices of business leaders, government representatives, social service agencies and school officials.

Denise was making connections among these people, many of whom were concerned about the same issues. She saw the need for networking and brokering needs and resources. She was finding out about the quality of life in Pasadena.

The first tangible result was a book published in 1984 called *Experiencing Pasadena—The Needs, Promises and Tasks of an American City*. After summarizing the pain of Pasadena and the structures and programs that offered "green shoots of hope," Denise made two strong recommendations:

1. Pasadena should not be allowed to become a polarized city, one part rich and one part poor.

2. We must give the highest priority to the needs of our young people.

Denise's report had such an impact on city leaders that many kept it at the front of their consciousness as they adopted policies and created programs. One of the city directors pinned sections of the book to his bulletin board.

And the All Saints Vestry authorized a permanent gift to

the city—an Office for Creative Connections based at All Saints with Denise as its first director. This office and its ongoing work would be the church's gift to the city of Pasadena in celebration of All Saints' Centennial.

OCC has become a major institution in the city over the last ten years. It is concerned with the quality of life for all Pasadena's citizens, but especially the poor and the children. Through roundtable discussions focusing on specific issues, through citizen input, and through connecting people with common concerns in progressive interaction, OCC has spawned two major initiatives.

The first of these was Day One, a program of drug and alcohol abuse prevention that began out of a roundtable discussion in 1987. A grassroots organization under the direction of Fran Neumann was created to provide leadership in five areas: alternative activities for youth; education and public information; law enforcement and safe neighborhoods; treatment and rehabilitation; and enlightened alcohol policy.

Begun with a grant of $5,000 from the City of Pasadena, the agency has grown via a $200,000 grant for three years from Kaiser Permanente, then a $2.76 million grant over five years from the Center for Substance Abuse Prevention of the federal Health and Human Services Department. Every parochial school has now adopted a curriculum on drug and alcohol prevention; and the city has an alcohol policy that Day One suggested for the use of the Rose Bowl, for problem liquor outlets, for underage drinking, and for the granting of conditional use permits.

Day One's theme is "Take Charge of Your Life; Take Care of Your Community." Perhaps its most important work is community organizing and empowerment to carry out this mandate.

Another book was published in 1986 based on research

done by Lorna Miller, who began as Denise's assistant and took over the direction of OCC when Denise and John retired from All Saints (and John from his job with the Braille Institute) and moved back east. This book, authored by Denise, was entitled *Growing Up in Pasadena—What Are Our Children Telling Us?* The research and writing were powerful enough once again to change the direction of a community. Among the topics were the early childhood experience; child abuse; drugs, alcohol and gangs; teenage pregnancy; and parenting skills.

OCC has learned to build hope and constructive alternatives into all its roundtable and grazing processes. The OCC methodology has had an influence far beyond the City of Pasadena. Denise and John Wood, in their newest retirement mode, have taken the listening/grazing/roundtable/consensus/action model to places such as Richmond, Virginia; Chicago; and Bermuda. They call this the "Pasadena Process," and the church which has the community as its parish and accepts the risk of community involvement is the connective tissue that makes the entire process work.

Prophetic leadership is not always combative leadership. The diverse congregation at All Saints has produced both combative and non-combative varieties over the years, and different situations require different approaches. The secret of the success of people like John and Denise is the spiritual perception they bring to their tasks. They are non-combative in their approach, yet their effectiveness at bringing people together around common issues to create new social paradigms is astounding.

They see a spark of divinity in every human being. That spark can arc its way among people to join them together in a network for constructive change. When you listen to people in a sacred way, without thinking about your agenda but all the while trying to discern theirs, you are really inviting that spark to work its way to the surface of their lives. Some of us have the spark of divinity buried way down deep. Our culture has taught us more about the sordidness of life than about the humane possibilities. Excitement for young people is more related to negative energy than positive. Guilt has more power in their lives than grace.

The Woods are not Pollyannas who fail to understand the dark side of life in individuals and in communities. Evil must be taken seriously. There is plenty of blame to go around. The Church more easily understands the corrosive effects of guilt in a human life, than the Church understands the powerful ferment of grace. We think that grace is an inert and impotent state of mind—a theological precept that is filed away in our consciousness, but that has no salvific effect on ourselves, much less on our circle of influence.

All Saints is a place where both guilt and forgiveness are taken seriously. When Jesus told the woman taken in adultery, after he refused to condemn her, to "Go and sin no more," he was emphasizing the transforming power of forgiveness.

The eucharist is a high moment in the life of every good Episcopalian. But if we go away thinking that we have been forgiven we are understanding only part of its effect. When people like John and Denise leave the altar rail, they appreciate that they have been forgiven, but they also have a spiritual concept that their community has been liberated. People are learning skills so that they can get better jobs. Children are seeing their neighborhood dentist for the first time in their lives. Young people are turning away from drugs and participating in a midnight basketball league instead. Poor people are taking responsibility for their neighborhoods. The democratic process is being revitalized.

"Go and sin no more" is a bit of an understatement.

The Church can be a community catalyst—a "catalytic converter" perhaps—that transforms the despairing statistics of urban life in the United States into green shoots of hope.

During the long dialogues that led to the programs described above, one of the participants turned to Denise and shared her view of the importance of the effort: "This is where the vision is kept." In order to turn the tide of decline in mainline American religion, and to turn the tide of polarization in our cities, we need a vision of a good society and a passionate spirituality.

How does a church draw two people of the caliber of Denise and John Wood into its orbit?

Basil Entwistle has written a book about this couple entitled *Making Cities Work—How Two People Mobilized a Community to Meet Its Needs*. In the foreword to that book, Don Miller cited two characteristics of the All Saints parish: integrity and prophetic vision.

This vision is a sacred embodiment of God at work in the life of a parish—which in the broad sense is the community in which we live. The Rector holds this vision up to us each week in the words of the Gospel reading and in the word of God from the pulpit. This vision invades our being each week in the eucharist, when we take into ourselves the power of Christ, broken and poured out for the life of the world.

So All Saints helps to create people like John and Denise Wood, because the integrity and prophetic vision of our Rector and our parish elicits from them their own gifts. People want to make an offering of their lives and talents when they understand that high calling to be the standard and the expectation.

And of course people like John and Denise Wood also create All Saints.

I remember a Vestry committee meeting that John was

chairing in the early days of my own involvement with the parish. He stated that on a particular issue under consideration he felt that the role of the Church was to be an advocate not for its own self-interest, but on behalf of the poor. I had never heard such words spoken with such integrity coming from a lay person. And those words strengthened my own career resolve to serve the poor.

George Regas creates a parish in which people who are committed to Christ can flourish. Perhaps that is his greatest gift to his staff and parishioners. His own compassion and vision sets the standard for the rest of us. And together we maintain the vision that is so vital to the welfare of our community. Like the Torah that is secure in its sacred place in the temple, we keep the vision in a sacred place at the center of our worship service.

When George preaches the gospel he holds out to us this vision, week after week. We revisit this vision and it nourishes our spirit and reshapes our lives. It is God's vision for God's children, and we are the stewards of its liberating power. When we come into its presence, our hearts are set on fire, for Christ's sake.

Teaching in the context of the celebration of the eucharist.

Chapter 14

The Inclusive Church

ALL SAINTS UNDER JOHN BURT and increasingly under George Regas had included women prominently in the leadership of the parish. But the issue of language was never addressed until a day in 1969 when George attended a Journey in Faith small group meeting. A parishioner named Margaret Sedenquist stated that she was offended by the masculine language of the Sunday morning service.

"I think you're overstating it, Margaret," George responded with some defensiveness.

Margaret pulled from her folder a series of 12 Sunday morning liturgies, with the male pronouns and references all underlined in red. Out of 100 gender references on an average Sunday, 97 were male.

"Am I, George?" Margaret asked.

But Margaret had more than statistics on her side. When her daughter Diana was two years old, Margaret had asked her, "What do you want to be when you grow up?"

Diana replied, "A doctor."

The conversation was repeated when Diana was six years old. But this time the reply was, "A nurse."

"Why the change?" Margaret asked.

"Oh Mommy, girls aren't supposed to be doctors!"

The use of words is a very powerful weapon for either good or evil, liberation or oppression. Words are not neutral. People such as Margaret had to shake the church into accountability for the expressions of faith which were so reflective of male-oriented and dominated society. George took her convictions seriously, and began to come to grips with his complicity.

At a 1970s Diocesan Convention in Los Angeles, Bill Rodiger of All Saints was serving as the chair of the Commission on Canons. The Canons at the time were loaded with hierarchical male language. Margaret Sedenquist was a lay delegate from All Saints who took the microphone to move that the Canons be rewritten to give equal consideration to women. The logistics of the undertaking would be massive, but Mr. Rodiger promised that his committee would work over the next year to have a recommended version ready for adoption at the next convention.

"Does that satisfy you, Mrs. Sedenquist?" Bill innocently asked from the podium.

"From you I'm not seeking satisfaction, Mr. Rodiger, only justice!" Margaret shot back.

Today Margaret and Bill and George Regas can give personal testimonies about the flow of liberation that emanates from the changing of oppressive and exclusive language. Women and men alike have been transformed by the power of words. Expansive language allows people to walk on some of God's beaches, where they were told they could never walk.

Despite John Burt's earlier statement in 1964 that women would never want to be priests, there were in the early 1970s many women knocking at the door of a priesthood that had been denied them by the national Episcopal Church. A few "irregular" ordinations had taken place without the sanction of church law prior to an important gathering of national church leaders in 1974. These leaders, including some bishops, lay people, clergy and women, met for three days in

Chicago to discuss a strategy for winning the battle for women's ordination. George Regas was among them. The battleground would be in Minneapolis in June of 1976, when the triennial General Convention of the Episcopal Church would take place.

At the conclusion of the Chicago meeting, George was elected chair of the newly-formed Coalition for the Ordination of Women. For the next two years he spent 50 percent of his time working throughout the nation to create an environment that was enlightened and supportive, and to line up the delegate votes that would be required. All Saints became the center of fundraising and strategizing. The undertaking was vast. Prophetic vision would have to be accompanied by logistical competence in order to succeed.

The vote in 1976 was very close, but the campaign was victorious. All Saints was solidly behind the effort, and there was unanimous support on the part of the Vestry. But the Diocese of Los Angeles was only narrowly supportive.

In 1975, George had welcomed to America a priest from Hong Kong, Jane Hwang, the first ordained woman in the worldwide Anglican communion. George invited her to celebrate the eucharist at All Saints, since she was, after all, a priest. The newspapers got wind of the story, before the event, and a contingent of priests unsuccessfully urged Bishop Robert Rusack to forbid the celebration. But when the worship service took place, parishioners were lined up out the door of the church to receive the bread of the eucharist from the Reverend Jane Hwang.

After 1976, the issue became more and more how to liberate ourselves from the traditional language of a masculine God ruling over a patriarchal church. To think of God as exclusively "Father" is not only to oppress women, but to rob all of us of the image of God as being both male and female. Great liberating power abides in the notion of God as our "Mother" also. So the replacement of exclusive language with expansive language, broad enough to contain a more meaningful expression of faith, continues to be a peace and justice goal of the parish. Hymns and scriptures and the traditional words of the liturgy are continually under review.

The effort is not just a pursuit of political correctness. People's lives are at stake. When we are successful at being expansive in our language, we hear from both men and women about the grace that floods back into their lives and about the deepening of their faith. Anne Peterson and a succession of working groups under her leadership have kept us at the task of inclusivity. The liturgy has sometimes been given over experimentally to the feminine side of God, and the spiritual enrichment offered by such a service has been dramatic. Liturgy is a powerful force for transformation in the tradition of All Saints Church.

The inclusivity movement toward acknowledging the rights of gay and lesbian members of the parish has been more recent, and has caused more of an internal trauma for the parish.

Mark Benson came from the home of an Iowa fundamentalist minister. He had a view of faith as an entryway into a "sinless" life—not a journey, but a static acceptance of a divine purity. Such a world view, as preached and practiced at the Oskaloosa Gospel Tabernacle, didn't allow for homosexual urges.

Nevertheless, at the age of 16 Mark confessed these feelings to his parents. They were very supportive of their son, but felt he needed professional help to overcome a personal flaw that "grieved the Lord's heart."

Phil Straw also came from a conservative religious home. His father was a Baptist preacher, and Phil was very scrupulous about basing his life in scripture. He was on a church staff himself as a licensed Baptist minister in New York City for five years. When he finally disclosed his homosexuality, even though he was celibate, his church expelled him from any leadership role. He came to Santa Barbara in 1973, where he worked as a hospital orderly for ten years.

Mark and Phil met in the fall of 1983, at a church conference conducted by Yale University's John Boswell and designed to help people of all sexual orientations to bring God and sexuality together, without denying the one for the sake of the other. In January of 1984 they pledged themselves to each other as partners for life. Phil moved to the Los Angeles area to be with Mark, and to become a member with him of All Saints Church.

They were not here initially to be advocates for anything, but simply because they loved the church and worship experience. In the spring of 1985 they participated with the Rev. Denis O'Pray in a group study on the incarnation. Denis brought up the gifts that gay people brought to the church, instead of curses. With this encouragement, a small group of parishioners began to meet to discuss how they could minister to the numbers of gays and lesbians, known and unknown, who were church members.

In the fall of 1985, with the church's blessing, the bulletin announced an inaugural meeting of a group that would later be called GALAS—Gays and Lesbians/All Saints. About 25 came to Dick White's home. Half were terrified of disclosure of their sexual orientation, and they wanted to meet regularly but privately off the church campus. Others wanted to be more open and aggressive, and they wanted to meet at the church. So the decision was made to have alternate meetings, a potluck in a parishioner's home and a discussion group at the church.

The group wanted to offer their support to the ministry of

All Saints, to be active in stewardship and outreach projects, for example. They also wanted to have a ministry of support to members of the parish who were gay or lesbian, many of whom were struggling with their sexuality and their faith, trying to sort their way through issues of rejection by family and society and the church.

The church staff was a bit nervous about the name GALAS, because of the unhelpful connotation of frivolity. Mark Benson would submit articles about upcoming meetings to the bulletin, and for the front page of the Sunday morning printed liturgy, where the editor would always spell out the name in full and omit the acronym. One of the tables on the lawn became a GALAS table to disseminate information to members, but also to straight parishioners who wanted to find out more about the true meaning of inclusivity.

In 1986 George met with Mark and Phil over breakfast. The issue of the blessing of their covenant by the church arose, and this serious possibility became a topic for periodic staff discussion. Progress was gradual. The champions for gay and lesbian rights were tenacious.

In 1987, Mark became the first openly gay person on the Vestry, where he became the spokesperson for GALAS in addition to the other considerable gifts he brought.

In the meantime, on a related front, the church was considering its response to the AIDS crisis. Bob Iles, a priest and member of the parish but not on the staff, began in 1985 to raise the issue with George and Denis O'Pray that the church had to become involved. Denis and George responded almost in unison: "What are you going to do about it?"

Bob was dispatched to a seminal conference in 1986 sponsored by Grace Cathedral in San Francisco on "The Church's Response to AIDS." He returned to Pasadena to convene a group that eventually grew to 40 to plan a next step of faith.

The issue of inclusivity for those suffering from a disease, outcast from society, and for those stigmatized by the Church because of their sexuality, was becoming a much more focused issue for the Rector and for the parish.

Bob Iles developed a liaison with the Pasadena Health Department and Betty Jean Prosser, a registered nurse and member of the department staff. She had started the Pasadena AIDS Consortium, and this networking was an invaluable boost as All Saints across the street made its way into action.

The first step toward a program of outreach was the installation of a phone line at the church to receive the calls of those who needed information and referral. People with AIDS in the San Gabriel Valley, with Pasadena at the western edge, had to go to AIDS Project Los Angeles for services. A group of volunteers emerging from the ranks of All Saints' task force would return messages daily. One of the urgent needs was for a local support group. Connie McCleary led the first small group, with many others to follow.

Albert Ogle was another priest in the Diocese of Los Angeles who was working on the Church's role in the crisis. Bob talked to him and to George about raising some foundation and government money to begin a formal organization, with Albert as the executive director. George responded with an enthusiastic endorsement: "Albert is the best fundraiser I know, next to me!"

A nonprofit was formed called the All Saints AIDS Service Center, with John Littlewood of the parish as the first chairman and Mark Benson as a member. Non-All Saints people and straight people were always included in the ministry, which was defined as an outreach to those suffering from a physical disease, not to people with any particular lifestyle or sexual orientation.

In November of 1988 a major symposium on "The Gospel

Imperative in the Midst of AIDS—Towards a Prophetic Pastoral Theology" was co-sponsored by our AIDS Center and by the Church Divinity School of the Pacific in Berkeley. This prestigious gathering of 100 people from around the country was a benchmark in the Church's growing acceptance of its leadership role. Bob Iles edited a book with the same name as the conference in 1989, a collection of the papers and responses presented at the symposium, which had an even broader impact.

The explosive expansion of the Center to become a major institution for serving the needs of hundreds of AIDS and HIV people in the San Gabriel Valley and beyond is an amazing chronicle of the power of religious faith when it is liberated by enlightened theology. The Center's board of directors, led by parishioner Peggy Phelps as chair, is considering a 1995 budget of about $4.6 million to support its work. A small part of this amount will be generated by their annual Posada, which, much like Union Station's Dinners-in-the-Park, is a powerful union of people for the spiritual transformation of the life of a community.

The development of this ministry of the AIDS Service Center became another stepping stone toward full recognition of the rights of gays and lesbians at All Saints. It attracted more and more gay and lesbian people to the congregation. Many of them brought great gifts and energy to the work of building a parish. They became active in outreach, Christian education, music, and stewardship. Unfortunately, many of them came to All Saints to die. They gave AIDS a human face.

All of this ferment of ideas and actions brought again to center stage the question of the blessing of same-sex unions. Society on the one hand castigated people for an irresponsible lifestyle, and on the other hand denied these same people the social structure that would allow them to celebrate and honor loving relationships and lifetime commitments.

George Regas at first suggested that a private ceremony for Phil and Mark in his office would be an important step toward inclusivity. But Phil and Mark wanted a public witness, and George knew they were right.

On November 11, 1990, George preached a sermon, "God, Sex and Justice," as historic and prophetic as the "Mr. President, The Jury Is In" sermon 20 years earlier. The justice issues were clear and were rooted in biblical interpretation and spiritual formation. The call to mobilize the parish for study and action and implementation was also clear. The healing and reconciliation that would flow from the blessing of same-sex unions would liberate the Church from centuries of oppression. The granting of the God-given right to millions of people to walk on God's beaches, where they had never been allowed to walk, would be one of the great, proud moments in the history of the Christian Church.

The lifetime fidelity of Mark Benson and Phil Straw was celebrated at a service of union on January 18, 1992. People young and old, gay and straight, vindicated after years of struggle, exuberant and contemplative, holding up colorful banners made for the occasion and holding back tears, joined in the event.

Mark would later reflect on Phil's behalf also: "This was the highlight of our lives here." It was a highlight of the lives of many of us who were privileged to be present.

Phil Straw died from AIDS in December of 1992. Mark, now 51 years old, has returned to live in Santa Barbara. It had been hard for him to be at All Saints after Phil's death. He misses the energy of All Saints. He misses the prospect of growing old together with his loved one. But for the present a measure of privacy and solitude seems appropriate.

One of the important concepts of life at All Saints is the concept of "gathering the faithful"—rich and poor, women and men, straight and gay, healthy and sick. All are invited, wherever they are on their journey, to come to the eucharist. One would think that this is the most non-controversial aspect of the ministry of All Saints Church. Hasn't the Church, down through the ages, always been "the Church of the open door"?

The sad fact is that the Church has traditionally been exclusive, and even more distressing is the reality that most of its focused exclusions have been based on an interpretation or a misinterpretation of the Bible. The Church is not yet what it was intended by God to be, and inclusivity is an idea in process with respect to socio-economic and religious and ethnic differences.

Despite the fact that we have miles to go, the spirit of inclusivity is in place and the progress has been monumental. Bishop Fred Borsch brought with him to the Diocese of Los Angeles in 1988 a theme of "Arms Out" for the embrace of all who can journey with us toward inclusivity. Our Bishop and our Rector have been a great national beacon of hope for an expansive Church. Our progress has been marked by memorable dramatic moments coming at the conclusion of long and sometimes agonizing periods of study and meditation. We understand inclusivity to be a justice issue, and champions have come forward to push us and pull us into conformity with God's values.

Chapter 15

Building a Parish

SHORTLY AFTER GEORGE ARRIVED at All Saints in 1967, he arranged for the parish leadership to go on a train ride to Redlands, about 60 miles east of Pasadena. Bill Rodiger recalls the journey. The train may have covered 100 miles, but George covered even more, working his way up and down the aisles, a nonstop express, listening and sharing and hugging.

George was building a parish, and the symbol of that train ride has continued for 28 years. All of us on George's staff, and many lay people as well, are keenly aware that we have been deputized to be parish-builders.

We work our way among the throng, listening and sharing and hugging.

There are many pitfalls in building a parish with the resources and outreach mission of All Saints.

One temptation is to think of the work of the Church as unrelieved glory. Even our failures can be poignant and designed to make us look good because of our perseverance in the face of overwhelming odds. Failures a few years after the fact may be remembered as noble. But in the midst of failure the sense is one of unredeemed loss. I remember the story of the person who complained to his psychiatrist that he always felt like a failure. The psychiatrist responded, "That's because you *are* a failure."

The temptation to glorify our failures is matched by the

temptation to glorify the work as always exhilarating. Sometimes people leave a Sunday morning service with the comment, "That was a glorious service!" But what goes into such a service? Does the Holy Spirit make it glorious by magic? Was it glorious when our devout band of collators was assembling the liturgy all Friday morning? Was it glorious throughout the last year of planning the music? Is the choir always on a spiritual high at their midweek practices?

Another pitfall is to take ourselves too seriously. All of our high-powered activity must be surrounded by humility and self-deprecating humor.

The Rector's Office is a nerve center of productivity presided over by the executive assistant to the Rector, Anne Peterson, or, as she calls herself, the "Rector Director." Anne has been at All Saints for 17 years, with her own right-hand person for all of that time, Lois Marski.

I said to George once, "I suppose Anne doubles your output. Even I could be effective if I had an Anne Peterson at my side."

He replied, "No, she quadruples it."

"If she quadruples your effectiveness, maybe she should be the Rector."

Only a person with a great sense of humor could bear the burdens that George Regas bears. Most of us around him for very long also learn how to maintain a light touch. Those of us who know George best understand this side of his personality. There is no finer pastor or prophet in the Episcopal Church. But he tells me that in his two unsuccessful attempts to become a bishop, everyone who interviewed him took into account all of his fundraising skills and preaching skills and leadership skills. But no one asked him about his ability to laugh at himself.

We really don't know whether we are making very much of

a difference in the flow of history. Our ignorance about final results doesn't diminish our intensity (in fact it increases it), but this not-knowing causes us to put an asterisk next to all of our heroics, with an explanatory footnote that reads: "We may have been wrong about this."

One of my professors used to tell me that the best theologians in the world are right only about 75 percent of the time. I suppose that the best prophets and social ethicists score even lower. But when my professor taught about any issue, he allowed for no alternative interpretations. He didn't acknowledge in the least that he might be mistaken. I confronted him once with what I thought was an obvious hypocrisy.

"How can you be so sure of yourself when even the best theologians are wrong 25 percent of the time?"

His matter of fact answer was, "I don't teach about that 25 percent." He was serious!

Congratulations. We at All Saints wish we could isolate our potential for failure so completely that we could just enter those arenas where we know all the correct answers in advance. We love to take risks, just as long as we know that success is guaranteed.

George Regas preaches and leads with all the force of his personality and his intellect. Many people are overwhelmed. A few consider him to be tyrannical. But he really doesn't feel that he has a monopoly on right causes. He knows better. He hopes he's right most of the time. The forceful presentation is at least in part an attempt to elicit forceful alternative presentations. Let's at least engage the issue together.

But let's allow a touch of humor and humility to lighten the process.

And a final temptation is to build a parish out of the high profile social action programs of the church and divorce them from the nuts and bolts of ecclesiastical life. Not every church buys a hotel on Skid Row, but every church visits the sick and teaches the Bible to the children. What makes All Saints distinct may have more to do with the high profile programs, but what makes us effective as a parish has more to do with visiting the sick and teaching the children. So we can't ignore these critical components of parish life.

You may think that when our staff gathers for its weekly meeting we spend most of our time talking about changing the world. Such intensity would make life at All Saints unbearable. Even those who are on the front lines in the struggle to change the world don't spend most of their time thinking about it.

The history of All Saints that we know about, beginning at least with Dr. Leslie Learned in 1908, tells us that someone expended a lot of effort successfully building a parish. That groundwork that has been laid is very important for our concept of social progress, to which we are so devoted, because we understand that progress is a matter of new uses of power.

Progress doesn't come about because of our impotence. God may choose the weak, and we are prime candidates, but God empowers us. We need thousands of people to give us about $2.5 million each year to carry on our work, not counting the other millions for our spin-offs like the AIDS Service Center, Young & Healthy, Day One, and Union Station. At one point in our Union Station history we needed 1,000 people to show up at a City Board of Directors meeting. At one point in our quest to create a non-violent city we needed 800 people to put their minds and bodies into the effort. You can be a solo prophet and cry out in the wilderness, and you may be absolutely correct in all your observations. You can be a martyr for a cause. And we thank God for the prophets and the martyrs.

But what if you actually want to reconcile the world to

God? Who's going to do the work? What if you actually believe that the Lord's Prayer is serious when it talks about God's will being done on earth? Who's going to prepare the highway for God to ride into the center of our lives and our neighborhoods?

We get the work done because we build a parish. Building a parish has pastoral, educational, liturgical, aesthetic, financial, and logistical components to it. For every hero and heroine mentioned in this book, there are at least a hundred other anonymous people at All Saints and in the community. They are anonymous to you, the reader, but they had better not be anonymous to those of us out in front trying to create a sanctuary for children or a non-violent city. We need to know the names and phone numbers of those people. They need to be collaborators with us in the creation of a new society.

Many people may appear to us to be on the fringes of life at All Saints. I think we would be surprised to know how much they believe in what we are trying to accomplish together. They are not leaders or spokespeople. They don't think of themselves as pioneers, because they aren't. Thankfully, not very many of them have their own agendas to present to us with the question, "What's the matter with your church?"

These people are just faithful "salt of the earth" people, and that phrase is chosen advisedly. For these people make our initiatives succeed or fail.

In the Sermon on the Mount, the salt of the earth is a name chosen by Jesus to describe the believers.

A graduating high school senior was accepted for admission to a prestigious university, despite a mediocre academic record. When he arrived on campus he met the admissions director and asked why he had been accepted. The admissions director responded, "We have 1,000 entering students this fall. When we asked on the application whether they considered themselves to be leaders or followers, you were the only one who said you were a follower. And we thought we needed at least one follower on campus."

At All Saints we depend on plenty of followers.

Gary Bradley is our priest in charge of pastoral work. He could do what he does at any church, theoretically, but he would himself die spiritually if he weren't doing his work in the context of a prophetic ministry. The purpose of his pastoring is to connect people to the outreach and nurturing sides of our program, for people can't be healthy in themselves if they don't in some way invest their lives for the good of the community. A parishioner is more likely to be healed when she is linked to a healing presence in the world. Pastoring is for the ultimate purpose of enabling.

The management staff at All Saints consists of a dozen people—half of them ordained clergy and half lay people. We are all pastors, especially to the people who are active in our particular programs. Jim Walker, for example, is primary pastor to the members of his choir. I am the pastor to people on my housing committees. We know as a staff that pastoring people can't be divorced from the success of our programs.

The pool of people who are in the pastoral care network consists of about 1,300 pledging units—families or couples or single people. The total number of people represented by these pledging units is over 3,000. Pastoring this many people has to be organized. It doesn't just happen because we run into Harry in the supermarket and have a nice chat with him.

Since Jim and I and four others of us on the management staff are lay people, we can't marry people or bury them, and there is what might be called a pastor override system where we bring specific needs to the attention of clergy on the staff. But for most pastoral needs, we serve the people who are related naturally to our areas of ministry.

"What if someone who serves as an usher is not a pledger, and hence not in the pastoral care network?" you might ask. That's easy. If you don't pledge, you don't usher. You are welcome to come to programs and to worship services and to the eucharist, of course. And if you die, we will have your memorial service, no questions asked.

But we can't build a parish around people whose only contribution is their time and energy, as important as these are. Pledge in proportion to your resources, tithe, pledge $1 a week, but pledge, or you won't find yourself in any leadership role at All Saints Church. You won't be an usher or a collator of the liturgy or a member of the Vestry.

This policy has less to do with greed on the part of the stewardship office, although they are a hungry bunch over there, and more to do with a concept of spiritual wholeness as taught by the Rector. There are nice churches where you can attend without being asked to pledge. All Saints is not one of them.

This policy also acts as a kind of filter for pastoral priorities. In a church which views the community as its parish, tens of thousands of people have some role to play in our broader mission. We don't consider them pledge prospects unless they consider themselves to be members of All Saints. We are responsive to human need wherever we find it, but we don't become proactive pastors to people unless they are pledgers.

It would be a tidy arrangement if each of us on the management staff knew all of the 100 families in our pastoral care cluster. Unfortunately, about 10 percent of our pledging families are unknown to anyone, at least by name. So these people are distributed among us at random, at least until we discover something about them that might put them in someone else's cluster.

Within each of our clusters, we can't possibly pastor all 100 family units. Some of these people we see naturally. Bob and Barbara Miller are active in housing issues, and I see them at least once a week. Pastoring is not automatic, but at least the opportunity is there. Of course Bob and Barbara are not good examples of the system, because everyone else on staff knows them also and they have their noses in everyone else's programs. That's fine, as long as I don't catch another staff person doing any out-of-bounds pastoring with my cluster members.

The idea is to provide pastoral care to the well along with the sick, both preventive and reactive. If something significant is happening in someone's life, such as a marital problem or a hospitalization or a crisis in faith, then that information is communicated up the line to the appropriate priest. If the information is noteworthy but not urgent, then the responsible member of the management staff types it into the computer. It becomes part of a pastoral care screen on each family in the parish, unless the information is confidential. Every comment typed in during a given week is then printed out on a comprehensive sheet and circulated to every member of the management staff.

The one exception to this rule is the Rector, who doesn't know how to turn the computer on. He has his staff type in the data. They quadruple his effectiveness.

The system doesn't work perfectly. It is a bit impersonal. Gary Bradley's job is to get a recalcitrant staff to be disciplined about following through. But when the system works, the quality of care is enlightened and very personal. Laypeople are involved in pastoring, which is essential in a growth church environment. And situations like the following are avoided:

I walked up to an elderly member of the parish whom I had met only once before as she was helping to decorate the church for Christmas one year. As I approached her, the name of her husband came to mind, and I was anxious to put my pastoral skills into action. A little knowledge is a dangerous thing. I blurted out, "Where's Herman this afternoon?"

"Oh, he died last week," she calmly replied.

There are two other critical components to the All Saints' scheme of pastoral care: the Parish Council and the Newcomer Ministers. These are groups of lay leaders (all pledgers, of course!) who meet with Gary Bradley each month. The Newcomer Ministers make phone calls to everyone who signs a visitor's pew card giving us their name and stating some interest in the church. You also will receive a call if you put a check in the offering plate and are otherwise unknown to us. The purpose is to move these people into participation in the life of the parish and into our membership class, to get them on our bulletin mailing list, and to establish at least some personal contact.

The Parish Council makes a few dozen routine telephone calls on pledging families each Monday evening, working their way down the long list. All will be called at least twice in the course of the year, and they will not be asked for money. Members of the parish seem to appreciate this "no-agenda" contact, which is usually just a brief pleasant chat. They are often surprised that someone cares how they are doing, and how they feel about their church. If any startling information is uncovered, it is entered into the computer or, if there is a crisis, passed immediately to Gary.

The Parish Council also responds if a staff member fills out a green "call request" form. Perhaps we are wondering why Joe hasn't been at church for a few weeks. Joe is not a member of our pastoral cluster, but someone should give him a call.

The homebound represent a special category of pastoral need. About 55 are identified in the parish family. Each one who wishes receives a visit once a month from one of our Lay Eucharistic Ministers, a specially-trained cadre of 15 lay people who are licensed to bring the eucharist into people's homes. At Christmas and Easter staff members divide up this list and take the eucharist, but the other ten months of the year the LEM's are activated.

And then we have those who are temporarily homebound or hospitalized. The goal is to visit everyone, in the hospital or in the home, at least once before any surgery, no matter how routine, and as necessary thereafter depending on the nature of the crisis, but at least weekly. Clergy receive the initial assignments and share with lay people subsequent visiting depending on the need.

Gary and his lay leadership also implement a rotating newcomer orientation meeting every Sunday in between the main services. Newcomers are invited to the Rector's Office for one of four sessions, depending on the Sunday of the month. The topics are the theology of All Saints, the nourishing ministries, the outreach programs, and a tour of the campus (which helps them to identify staff, places around campus and programs).

Those who are interested can then sign up for a seven-week Covenant Class, coordinated by Tim Safford three times a year, leading to confirmation by the Bishop, or general membership at All Saints, or transfer of membership. No one becomes a member without a financial commitment, and without at least prayerfully considering a tithe.

All Saints brings in about 250 new people each year through the Covenant Class process, but we lose about 100 through death, moving away, attrition, or protest. A large and politically active parish carries more risk than most in the last two categories. The challenge of incorporating the new members is immense, but vital to the implementation of our parish goals.

And part of incorporation is financial stewardship. We challenge people to tithe, and we ask those who do tithe to tell their stories publicly. People who are among our scores of canvassers in the fall are encouraged to share their own stories—not just how much they give, but why, and how their lives are transformed through generosity. Our Rector is of the persuasion that the happiest people in the world are those who give away the most money, proportional to their resources. We have a lot of anecdotal data to prove the thesis.

Being able to talk about money is a sign of spiritual maturity. It is also a sign of a church that is aggressive and successful with fundraising. We all wish our prayers alone would usher in the Kingdom of God. Maybe someday they will. In the meantime, we need lots of money, and we are respectfully aggressive about getting it. The best stewardship is pastoral and spiritual in nature. The annual canvass, perfected over many years by many of the best people in our parish, is carried out with great care and good humor.

The challenge of pastoral care is immense, also. We might wish that we didn't have to be so organized and computerized. The system is not perfect, and even if it were, the implementation is not perfect. But at its best, the system is a powerful tool for caring for people, and for enlisting them in the ministries of the church where they can make a difference.

George Regas and his earliest clergy staff: John Davis, Bill Rankin, Charles Cadigan and Huston Horn.

1994 All Saints staff at an all day retreat.

Chapter 16

Education for Ministry

IN 1938, KEN AND BETTY RHODES were married at All Saints Church. They had been occasional attendees of another Episcopal parish nearby, but they were from prominent Pasadena-area families who believed in big weddings. All Saints had the only church in town in those days that could accommodate the guest list.

Frank Scott was the Rector, and he came to know Ken and Betty in a more significant way on a train ride to the east coast. They had begun to attend more regularly, but their involvement was still nominal. You can't build much of a parish unless you capture people for a cause. People need a handle to grab to pull themselves on board, or else they are forever standing at the edges of parish life, missing out on the possibilities for spiritual growth and a liberating engagement with the power of God. Dr. Scott asked them somewhere in Missouri if they wanted to teach Sunday School.

Ken and Betty were raising a family just then, and they were too busy. "Maybe in a couple of years," they said, and Dr. Scott made a note of their response.

Two years later the phone rang at the Rhodes residence on Chula Vista. Ken was heard to exclaim, "We said what?"

So for the next 13 years Ken taught the sixth grade boys and Betty taught the sixth grade girls. They are not sure what impact they had on the children. But they remember coming home from church each week and having a beer.

In 1948, Ken became the Senior Warden of the Junior Vestry, which was as high as you could go in the church hierarchy as a young layperson. That was also the year that Ken, who was an attorney in Los Angeles, made an important decision. His father had died and left the growing Rhodes family an inheritance. Ken had graduated as a young man from the Thacher School in Ojai, California, and he had been listening to the preaching of Frank Scott for about a decade, and he had been influenced by a particular aunt. All of these forces had imbued him with a republican spirit of assuming some responsibility for the betterment of one's community. This was a "habit of the heart" that encouraged the notion of civic duty. Since the inheritance had given the Rhodeses some discretion about how they might use their time, Ken decided that he would give away one-third of his professional "billable hours" to worthy causes (not counting Sunday School). His church and a nearly endless list of nonprofit organizations have benefited from this arrangement up through the present day.

Frank Scott used a note pad rather than a computer to keep track of the pastoral needs and responses of his congregation. But his attention to detail and genuine caring are still a model for how to build a parish.

If you don't educate and pastor and listen to people, they will never incorporate themselves into your church or your cause, no matter how worthy.

Just as everyone on the management staff and our key lay people are pastors, we are also incorporators. We have our antennae out every day, in every conversation, at the market and on the airplane, sensing the needs and desires of people who are at least marginally related to our church, or even more importantly part of our cluster. We consider these needs and desires to be sacred expressions.

George Regas can personally testify to the importance of casual contacts. He was on a plane, instead of a train, sitting next to a man he vaguely recognized. "Don't I know you?" he asked.

"Yes, you're the Rector of my church," responded the man. "But I don't come very often."

"Why don't I see you every Sunday?" asked George.

"Well, there are a few things I don't like about the church."

"Give me a for instance."

"Well, there's you, for instance!"

"Oh, I see," said George, grateful that he wasn't on a cross-country train ride.

You have to start somewhere when you want to build a parish, and even though some leads aren't as promising as others, listening to people is, in a sense, more important than the content of what they say. This man actually became much more involved in parish life prior to his death from AIDS. When his death was imminent, he asked George to conduct his memorial service.

Just as listening to our parishioners—our customers—is of critical importance, the way we address them is also important. Our standard is one of excellence and caring. Whether they are receiving the weekly "Saints Alive" bulletin in the mail or the printed liturgy Sunday morning, whether they are participating in a small group or a forum or a worship service, we want the offering we make to them to be thoughtful and well done in every detail.

Huston Horn, a priest at All Saints in the 1970s, set the standard for a high-quality weekly bulletin. Not only was it proofread twice to be free from error, but it was crackling with humor and winsome in its invitation to participate in the programs of the parish. I was Huston's successor as the bulletin editor. On more than one occasion I had difficulty living up to Huston's standards, but one occasion stands out above the rest.

We always publish the prayer list so that parishioners can remember the sick and those who have died. The distinction is important. But one week I listed someone as deceased who was actually not quite dead as we went to press. When the bulletin was printed, at considerable expense, and ready for mailing, all 4000 copies, Don Perry noticed the error. What to do? Don took a magic marker and dutifully went through every copy to blot out the name. But as we solved one problem, we created another. Inside the back page was a picture of our Vestry candidates. The black ink that Don was applying was giving one of them, who happened to be a woman, a mustache. So a few hours into the process, we went to Plan C, which was to reprint the entire edition.

This is our style at All Saints, and some people criticize us for being too "performance-oriented." But over the years a lot of people have been ennobled by the way in which we value their presence with us. The church is competing with an array of other promoters in society, most of whom have much less to offer than the church but have much greater resources and skill. We are also promoters, without apology. We are competing for the hearts of our parishioners, trying to set them on fire, for Christ's sake.

Our biennial "Festival of Life" conference is a presentation of resources to the larger community, which we consider to be our parish. It is a sophisticated evangelistic tool for parish development and for making a substantial offering, without obligation, to people who are unchurched in the Pasadena area. As is true of so much that our parish has done, a layperson was the force behind the first Festival. Russ Reid, working with a Caring Committee, provided the ideas, the energy, and the financial guarantees that made the project a success.

Psychologists and educators and theologians come together to offer workshops to help people wherever they are on their journey into a more meaningful expression of life. Our invitation is also there, of course, to consider faithful, engaged and pledging membership in our parish family.

Tim Safford is in charge of our overall Sunday morning experience at All Saints, among many other responsibilities. His job is to make sure that all who come, from the newcomer to Ken and Betty Rhodes, have a gratifying experience with us, from the time they park their car until the time they leave the campus.

Tim takes his responsibility very seriously. We are consciously trying to be a growth church, which the ecclesiastical commentators tell us is not probable for a mainline liberal congregation. Our theology is akin to Mae West's philosophy: "Too much of a good thing is terrific!"

Tim wrote a memo to the staff this past spring that reflects our approach:

> *This past Palm Sunday, 1,600 people worshiped at All Saints. A record! It was an extremely moving service. We should prepare for new attendance highs for Maundy Thursday, Good Friday, Holy Saturday, and Easter Sunday. As always, our services will be beautiful, moving, and an opportunity to share with many our liturgy. Please attend Thursday to plan and envision our greatest Easter ever.*

He didn't even put an exclamation point at the end, because this was a routine memo around All Saints. We want everything to be "extremely," and the "greatest" as a matter of course. When I pointed out to Tim that the greatest Easter ever was probably the first one, he predictably responded, "There is nothing that can't be improved upon."

This is a risky arrogance that is in a strange way ennobling to people. We are engaged in the business of resurrections, transformations, paradigm shifts of grand proportions. We are trying to change the way all of us think and act. We are trying to save our planet and ourselves. And this demands a competence that helps people to understand that we are not "playing" church.

Of course, style without substance would be worse than no style at all. But we believe God has given us the substance, if we can honor its importance.

Under the staff direction of Gary Hall and his Adult Education committee, a curriculum for adults tries to maintain a balance between communicating information and nurturing personal growth. Intellectual exploration includes scriptural content, literature and poetry which relate to faith, and current events which raise questions of moral development. "Christianity 101" is set alongside the opportunity to hear prominent spokespeople for causes and theologies, whether or not we agree with them. Spiritual direction is available through a year-round array of small groups for life-sharing and faith-sharing.

Our small group program received its first inspiration from a wonderful parish family named Sabini. Bob Sabini was the president of a mining company. He and Cathy had three wonderful children. The parents last attended All Saints in June of 1972. They were killed in an airline crash in Europe the following week. George Regas became a temporary guardian for the youngest child, and Nancy Casad, a registered nurse and a member of the parish, lived in their home as a caretaker until other arrangements could be made.

As a memorial to them a program of "Sabini Groups" was launched, for sharing among parishioners and to introduce new people to the parish. Over the next several years they had a strong impact on many who participated. Growth in faith at All Saints is a matter of being taught, but also a matter of sharing. Every parishioner has a different journey. Only one-third of our members were raised as Episcopalians. We have much to learn from each other.

Over the years our small group programs have taken many different forms. We have Journey in Faith book studies, Bible studies, Lenten groups, faith-sharing groups, Covenant Class small groups, Education for Ministry programs, and a host of support groups for people with specific needs. An additional emphasis of recent years has been to incorporate a sharing time, or a devotional time, into some of the program and task groups of the parish. When people meet to launch an outreach program, for example, or to prepare a Church School curriculum, we try to build in an educational or a sharing component. Many parishioners do not have the time or disposition to attend a separate small group. Whatever nurture they receive must be integrated into their cause-oriented engagement with All Saints.

Jim Walker and Tim Howard of our music staff direct two adult choirs. Part of one of their mission statements reads as follows:

> We are dedicated to providing a mutually supportive fellowship for all choir members, reflecting the All Saints belief in the dignity and value of the individual. We intend to act as ambassadors of the All Saints message of peace and justice for all.

And you thought choirs were just interested in producing beautiful music. That concept is also part of the Coventry Choir's reason for being. But the linkage to the spiritual formation and internal well-being of choir members, and the complementary linkage to the peace and justice outreach ministry of the church, is uniquely worthy of note. The choir experience is to be an occasion for incorporation into the life of the church. Choir members are to be nurtured and pastored, by Jim and Tim and by each other. The goal is to balance program accomplishment with the growth of an individual soul.

When our parish programs are part of a symbiotic network, then each parishioner can vicariously participate in the work and worship of the rest of us. I cheer the choir in its beautiful ministry of music, and I also sense its presence when I am serving a meal to a hungry person. The result is a mutually-uplifting fellowship.

The leadership of George Regas has created an inclusive church with this kind of integrity and mutuality.

The primary test of incorporation is whether people are involved themselves in carrying out the work of the church, not just attending the programs that others prepare. This involvement can be with the infrastructure of the congregation—ushers, acolytes, Altar Guild, Church School, Parish Council, Women's Council, and a host of other program groups—or with the "Seeds of Hope" that provide outreach opportunities.

Tim Safford and Marty Coleman and their lay leadership publish a Seeds of Hope catalog of opportunities a few times a year. Each page outlines a specific action that a person can take to work for peace and justice—knitting a sweater for a baby at Union Station or tutoring a Central American refugee or being a volunteer at the AIDS Service Center.

We don't really consider people "incorporated" until we see them filling up the ranks of the hundreds of "doers" at All Saints Church. Education and ministry, action and reflection, resurrection of self and empowerment of others—these are the balances for youth and adults that make All Saints a vigorous parish.

The people who come to All Saints come with different

expectations. Some are lifelong church people who settle in the Pasadena area, some are attracted to our liturgy and worship and music, some sign on to an issue or bring their own agendas for social change, and some are simply wounded people who see All Saints as an inclusive fellowship where they might be restored to wholeness. People lose their way into our church, and if we don't mind them, they lose their way out.

We lose people when we don't succeed in providing a common education so that we can have a common discourse; we don't attend to their pastoral needs; we don't take the time to listen to them; we don't engage them in at least one of the programs of the parish.

The rite of baptism is the gateway to incorporation. It is your statement, even if you are an infant without the words to articulate your innate faith, or even if you are an adult without the language of religious devotion, that you are open to the Spirit of God. You want to be incorporated into the fellowship of Christ.

We take that statement of faith at face value, and we apply the lay and staff energy of the congregation to build a parish around that faith.

Dick Gillett reminded me of the staff meeting long ago when we were interrupted by an urgent request from Lorraine Peyton, the Rector's assistant at the time. A man hitherto unknown to us had dropped in and demanded to see a priest immediately. George was summoned and the rest of us waited with anticipation while staff proceedings were suspended.

About 15 minutes later, George returned to tell us the story of this man who had a request so unique that we could think of no other such person in our collective memory of ecclesiastical history. He wanted to be "unbaptized!"

George told him that Episcopalians had no rite to allow for

the unbaptism of an individual. But in unpacking the reasons for this deterioration of faith, George at least understood the man's dilemma. We all felt some affinity for the poor soul. And that solidarity was a sufficient basis for the man to enter a liberation mode that had been missing in his life for a long time.

Some day we may have to invent a rite for unbaptizing a person. People usually just drift away without any closure or acknowledgement. But for now—and on into the next millennium—we are busy with the task of educating people for ministry, and incorporating them into the life-giving fellowship of All Saints Church.

Archbishop Desmond Tutu leading a worship service for the children.

Chapter 17

A Sanctuary for Children

ONE TUESDAY at our regular weekly staff meeting I poured myself a glass of Tang left over from the prior Sunday's Church School program. We serve Tang and cookies as refreshments for the children. As I took a sip I commented on the watery nature of the concoction. Someone had skimped on the orange powder. A passerby within earshot responded, "That's okay. It's for the children."

This person meant by this unwitting remark that preschoolers usually don't complain about their drinks lacking flavor. He certainly had no idea that his innocent comment would make its way into a discussion of the priority of children and family life at All Saints.

The church, Tang included, is for the children, who are otherwise the most underserved members of our society. They are the most inarticulate and least well-organized lobby for education and health care, for family support and Christian education. Yet their needs are more significant than those of any other constituency of the government or of the church.

The church's concern for peace and justice on the one hand and pastoral care and education on the other converge in the offering we make to our children. Children are uniquely situated at this time in the history of civilization. They embody our best hopes for a world that may some day celebrate the dignity of all of God's people. They also are the principal victims in a world that has turned ugly with prejudice and violence.

Young people are under siege in our society. The statistics and the anecdotal material are overwhelming, and we are at a crossroads in our culture as to whether we might simply abandon an entire generation.

Pasadena is far from being a place without resources, programs, and hope. Yet even in this City of Roses the picture is ominous. Of the 22,500 students in our public school system (which includes the children of Pasadena, Altadena, and Sierra Madre), 11,700 are from low-income families; 9,800 live with only one parent or in a group home; 9,000 participate in the free lunch program; 5,600 speak limited English; 5,200 receive some form of government financial assistance; and 7,000 are from families that lack health insurance.

Dwayne Dawson, Kristin Neily and Stephanie Naifeh lead our efforts with the involvement of a host of committed lay people. Our goal is to make All Saints a safe and nurturing place for kids—a "Sanctuary for Children." We are prone to be an "adult" place because the issues we deal with so often require maturity.

But peace and justice are not just "adult" issues. Our children have more at stake in the struggle to preserve our planet than we do. So Dwayne and Kristin and Stephanie make sure these issues pervade our programming for everyone from the Crib Room on up.

A curriculum is in place from pre-school through senior high that maintains a balance between content and process, teaching and listening. The days when we could just present a block of material and ask children to memorize it are over, in our public schools and in our church schools, whether we like it or not. At All Saints we mostly like it, because our children are humanized by a more interactive and dialogic teaching/listening process.

So a varied program is in place under the leadership of staff and numerous lay committees. Minisingers, Mastersingers, Troubadours and Acolytes, a Seekers Class for youth confirmands, Senior and Junior High Connection groups meeting on Sunday mornings and weekday evenings, camps and peace trips and service projects—these represent some of the program handles that incorporate young people into the life of the church.

We don't have to make our kids religious. They are more naturally spiritual than the rest of us, because they have a more immediate and untainted connection with their source—at least for a while. That is why toddlers are in awe of life. They sense a connection with the earth, with animals, with strangers, and with other human beings that speaks of mutual sacred origins. They have a greater ability to integrate reality than adults have, after corrosive cultural processes have interrupted our innate link to the creator God.

The old method of teaching where the exclusive emphasis was on disconnecting from life and "paying attention to religion" accentuated a process of compartmentalization and contributed to the "hurried child," scurrying from one compartment to another—family, school, friends and church. The results have been disastrous for our families and our culture.

We also understand that we can't create a safe place for the children of our parish without pastoring our families, and without reaching out to all the children in our wider community. So such programs as Project Safe Place, Brothers Making a Difference, Pasadena Family Center, Penny Lane Group Homes, the Praises of Zion/All Saints Summer Junior High Camp, and the Coalition for a Non-Violent City are all on our agenda, when it comes to the welfare of our own youth. Healthy children can't be sequestered away from a dysfunctional family or society.

One of the great blessings of the acquisition of the north property in 1965 was the opportunity to create an All Saints Children's Center one year later, in the newly-built Scott Hall. The Center now spans both sides of Euclid Avenue and provides day care five days a week to 130 children from infants to age five.

Director Myrna Shadley and her staff and board are dedicated to providing an affordable, high quality developmental program in an atmosphere that reflects the social, ethnic and cultural diversity of the surrounding community. Children discover compassionate ways of dealing with each other and the world. Approximately 30 of the children receive tuition assistance, and 25 are considered "at risk" due to poverty, neglect and abuse, homelessness, disability, or prenatal drug effect. Recently Huntington Memorial Hospital helped the Center expand into a new space across the street, to accompany the burgeoning demand and the hospital's own need for increased child care provision.

Another program for young people is also community-based, in our wider parish. It represents one of the most innovative approaches to solving the crisis in children's health care. The 1986 study on *Growing Up in Pasadena—What Are Our Children Telling Us?* led to roundtable discussions hosted at All Saints, under the direction of Lorna Miller, and focused on the health of Pasadena's youngsters.

Lorna had become the director of the Office for Creative Connections when Denise Wood retired. She has matched the dedication and skill of her mentor with her own stellar contributions to Pasadena's welfare.

Listening to community leaders and grassroots citizens, and

networking with some of the agencies that were tackling different aspects of the children's health care issue, led to some astounding results.

Lorna and Dr. Don Thomas, a parishioner and emergency room physician, convened a group of experts, some from the church and most from various agencies in the community. They met for two years to come up with a model that seems so simple and powerful, one wonders why every city doesn't put it into operation.

The school nurses in the Pasadena Unified School District were unable to meet the challenge of providing health care to underserved children, especially those from families with no health insurance. The ratio of children to nurses, Lorna had discovered, was 1,200 to one! Yet Pasadena is a community rich with hundreds of doctors, dentists, pharmacists and psychologists. Surely there would be a way to bring the people with resources together with the people with needs in a beneficial exchange.

So a program called Young & Healthy was born, standing alongside Day One as the second major OCC creation to bless the lives of hundreds of people in the wider parish. The idea behind Young & Healthy is to enlist professional health care providers to offer one child a week, or a month, free medical attention. The school nurses and Young & Healthy volunteers would identify needs and arrange appointments and transportation. The challenge for Don Thomas was to convince his physician colleagues to volunteer a fixed portion of their time.

So Don and Lorna arranged for a series of salmon dinners at Don and Sonia Thomas' home. The idea sputtered along for awhile, with a certain nervousness on the part of the professionals about what they were getting themselves into. By Christmas of 1990, 25 physicians had signed up; by June of

1991, 90 were on board; and today 130 professional health care providers have agreed to see at least one patient a month in exchange for salmon and immortality.

Mary Donnelly-Crocker became staff with Lorna for the program, which now also employs a case manager, Laura Diego, to follow up with the children and their families. The Irvine Foundation contributed $120,000 for three years' operation.

The school nursing offices made 227 referrals in the first year, 625 the second, 1,200 the third, and more than 2,000 in the 1993-94 school year. The program began in the 1990-91 school year in three grade schools. Today it operates in all 30 of the public schools, including the high schools, in the Pasadena Unified School District.

With follow-up care and some family intervention and counseling, the program has changed the lives of entire households. The stories of children, not just overcoming an ailment or having a tooth pulled, but having their perspective on life changed for the better, are stories that overwhelm the emotions.

Fifteen-year-old Patti, for example, arrived at school with a pronounced rash on her two cheeks and a terrible case of osteomyelitis, an infection of the bone, due to an untreated ingrown toe nail. She was referred to one of Young & Healthy's volunteer pediatricians. After several visits and many lab tests, the rash on the face was diagnosed as discoid lupus and treatment began, with Young & Healthy purchasing the proper medication. The pediatrician arranged for surgery on the toe and extensive follow-up care.

Ten-year-old Betty was referred to one of the volunteer dentists after she complained about a toothache. Her mouth was so badly infected that the dentist put Betty on antibiotics for two weeks before she could even begin to work on the teeth. Eventually ten teeth were extracted.

The children themselves are more eloquent using their own words of thanks.

> *Dear Dr.: Thank you for attending to me, cause the birth mark I had caused a lot of embarrassment. You did a beautiful job, you could barely notice the line.*

> *Dear Dr.: Thank you for helping me get new friends. I am very happy because I played with Susan for a short period of time, but it was the best 5 min. of my life.*

Young & Healthy is not merely a matter of providing physical care, as important as that can be in itself. Just as Union Station is a sacred place, a doctor's office or a dentist's chair can be a place where people meet God—in the face of a hungry and homeless person or in the eyes of a child with a rash.

Don Thomas, the champion along with Lorna of Young & Healthy, says, "We want resource people who have fire in their eyes."

Don continues, "Our problem in Pasadena is not lack of health services. We can solve the problem if we simply widen the door of every doctor's office and hospital office."

The spread of the Young & Healthy model to neighboring communities and states is now a priority for Lorna's time, if only she had more of it. But part of the promotion takes place through the inspiring work of Dr. Philip Porter, the director of Healthy Children, a program administered at Harvard University's Division of Health Policy Research and Education. Dr. Porter writes, "Lorna Miller, Don Thomas, Mary Donnelly-Crocker, George Regas and the rest of the Pasadena Health Coalition did not look toward Sacramento or Washington for a solution to their problem. They looked, instead, inside themselves, inside their community, inside the people who care most."

Without realizing the theological significance, perhaps, Dr. Porter has touched on a theme of the New Testament that we often overlook. The Kingdom of God, Jesus said, is within us.

George Regas carries out his work at All Saints with the foundational belief that within each person on his staff and within each parishioner, a "Kingdom of God" idea waits to be born. We honor and nurture each other because we have a divine and creative contribution to make to the ongoing work of our creator God.

George's role is not to produce all the ideas, nor to carry them out. He does produce and carry out more than his share. But his greatest contribution for 28 years has been to create an expectation within this All Saints community of faith, an expectation that some ideas could emerge to make all of us famous, all of us champions, all of us prisoners of hope. And the greatness of these ideas can be measured by the devotion and generosity they inspire in each of us.

The idea of All Saints as a "Sanctuary for Children" is surely one of the greatest, because it opens up to children both within the community and within the immediate parish family some transforming possibilities. Young people have a spiritual home and a caring support base. Pre-school children enjoy a weekday environment of warmth and challenge. And school children experience the affirmation that a generous society can bring to their vulnerable lives.

God's most beautiful people, our children, are walking on some of God's most beautiful beaches.

Chapter 18

Just a Country Preacher

LEONARD BEERMAN, affectionately called All Saints' Rabbi-in-Residence because of his collegiality with George and with the congregation, visited on a Sunday morning for one of his frequent teaching assignments. He addressed the Rector's Forum and recounted the story of his and George's visit to the Paris peace talks. When he repeated George's "aw shucks" introduction of himself to the American Ambassador as "just a country preacher," the Forum crowd roared with laughter.

George Regas is many things. He is a prophet, a pastor, and a preacher, but not of the unsophisticated hillbilly variety. He is also the CEO of a huge corporation. With 44 staff people and a budget approaching $3 million a year, the enterprise would be large enough. But when you factor in the time of many hundreds of volunteers, a few of whom seem to be at the church full time, the person power is enormous. Even at minimum wage, the dollar value of services rendered would make All Saints a Fortune 500 enterprise.

Riding herd over all this activity is a Vestry led by the Senior Warden, John Sweetland. John is representative of a large group of laypeople at All Saints, including both men and women, who are eminently successful professional and civic leaders. They take great pride in their career achievements in business, law, medicine, education, and government.

John also runs a 20-million-dollar-a-year corporation. And he chairs the board of Sheldon Jackson College in Sitka, Alaska, which consumes half his time. He is accustomed to making a difference with his life. And that is why he finds himself at All Saints. While he disagrees with George on some issues, he represents a core of support at the heart of the parish that has become convinced that the religious community is the only hope for a fading urban America. We must continue to evolve as a parish to be worthy of our leadership role.

These lay leaders are attracted to All Saints by George's view of the role of a church. George calls himself a "secular man who loves Jesus." He is a political as well as a spiritual animal. His father used to wake him up in the morning with the admonition, "See if you can make something of yourself today!"

George has made something of himself—and something of his church—and in the process he has changed the moral landscape of our society. So people who are similarly motivated to make a fundamental difference with their lives are eager to find an avenue for this endeavor. Without forsaking the realm of personal morality, about which George preaches frequently, the realm of public morality is also opened up for scrutiny and decisive action. At All Saints we believe we are the creators of public morality, and not the victims of it.

George Regas' faith integrates the world of the spirit with the "real" world of work and stress, success and laughter. This faith is a spirituality firmly grounded in the earthiness of life.

George sees the person of faith as one who lives a vigorous, authentic, and passionate life. He believes that the community of faith is a powerful agent of human transformation. In a time when people have become numb to the pain and disasters of the world, he awakens a deep sense of the interconnectedness of life and an understanding of how compassion for others is directly related to passion in our own lives.

A public corporate leader like John Sweetland grieves over the moral climate of urban America, in part because he is a good Christian, and in part because he is a successful businessman. In partnership with George Regas, he can deal with his grief by seeking personal solace, forgiveness for his complicity, and a platform for changing that moral climate. When a church can offer that holistic vision to a parishioner, including the possibilities for both personal and corporate transformation, then parishioners respond with the best leadership qualities and the deepest devotion to a cause that they can muster.

These people share the viewpoint that Grace Hall expressed when she visited the Anglican Cathedral in Nairobi, Kenya, a few years ago. As she was leaving she told the priest that she was a member of All Saints, Pasadena, California, U.S.A.

He replied, "Isn't that George Regas' church?"

And Grace said, "No. That's my church. George Regas is my Rector."

John Sweetland, like the rest of the Vestry and the rest of the parish, thinks that this is his church in the same way.

So this book is not a litany of "George did this…George did that." If anything, I have underplayed his pivotal role in many of the programs of All Saints Church for the sake of emphasizing a more important component in his ministry—the empowerment of the laity.

One of the stunning realities of life at 132 North Euclid is the engagement of people whose skill and commitment and generosity are overwhelming. People whose time in the corporate world is valued at hundreds of dollars an hour consider their role at All Saints to be their most fulfilling, most creative, and most challenging. Their innovative greatness comes to the surface in the context of a community of faith.

One of the many ways to put into perspective this incomparable ministry is to think of the beaches where God's children are walking today, in part because of this country preacher, George Regas.

People in South Africa are free. The cold war is over. Local leaders of the Jewish, Islamic and Christian faiths are together on a peace journey. Hungry and homeless and addicted citizens are receiving food and housing and rehabilitation. The unemployed and the underemployed in Pasadena have a chance to increase their skills. Farmworkers are more nearly able to support their families. People with AIDS are receiving care. Children are playing and learning in an environment of warm hospitality. Policies that contribute to drug abuse prevention and a less violent community are in place. Teenagers are playing basketball at a church gymnasium instead of hanging out at the neighborhood liquor store. Public school students are receiving free health care. Gay men and women are able to join together in a covenant that affirms the family values of love and human dignity. Rich and poor are overcoming barriers and stereotypes. Black and brown and white are joining in a community coalition. Women are priests and brilliant leaders in a communion that has existed for centuries without the benefit of their full offering of themselves. People who gave up on the church as being a marginal player in the creation of the public good have begun to reconsider the power of prayer and belief and hope.

If anything, this recitation is too brief and understated. Of course, the work remains in progress. Many others have been our colleagues in these struggles for peace and justice. That is part of the glory of the past three decades. And many others even prior to that have prepared All Saints to be the church it is today. We also believe that its greatness still lies in the future, under new management, but still an instrument of God in the pursuit of peace and justice.

George Regas has taught many of us that these global issues are not as intimidating as the power of love let loose in a world that is starving for the good news of the gospel of Jesus Christ. Like the leaders of the first century church, many of us at All Saints are comfortable with the idea of meeting with ambassadors and presidents, corporate chieftains and power brokers. We include them in the wider parish of an expansive church, because these people also are broken and in need of the healing power of forgiveness. Those with the trappings of wealth and power are also among the wounded victims of modern civilization. And they have their unique gifts to bring to the altar for the sake of the renewal of the world.

When our church ventured to Skid Row, many people spoke to us about the impact that the brazen display of violence and human exploitation might have on our delicate psyches. I responded to one such well-intentioned adviser:

"Have you ever encountered the brazen display of compassion?"

When you turn the tables on evil and invade a world of utter degradation with hope and dignity, you really do create new possibilities for goodness. Not without trauma, and not without humiliation. If you want to avoid the risk of these realities, you might want to avoid most of what the Gospel writers tell us about the ministry of Jesus.

But just to summarize the impact that All Saints has had upon its global community is to tell only half the story. A whole generation of young people in our congregation has been raised up in the context of hope. What a transforming difference that makes in a person's life! Even some of us too old for optimism have had second thoughts about the course of civilization. Perhaps there is a role for the Church in reconciling the real world to a real God after all. Perhaps we can be the *tikkun olam*–the menders of the world–that Rabbi Beerman and Rabbi Ragins tell us we are meant to be.

The story of All Saints begins and ends with "hearts on fire." George Regas in the pulpit has called us to love and serve the Lord with all of our being, and we are uplifted and consumed by this enterprise of sharing. An emancipating approach to life beckons each of us from wherever we find ourselves on the journey of faith. God often looks for us where we are, at the same time that we are off trying to meet God someplace else. But when we do meet God in the eucharist, our hearts are set on fire, for Christ's sake. And the inner transformation is even more remarkable than the outward effect.

The deeply spiritual journey inward is all of a piece with the deeply spiritual journey outward. This liberating concept is what George Regas has taught us, and lived out for us before our eyes.

I am reminded of the story of the disciples on the road to Emmaus, on the afternoon of the resurrection. They encounter Jesus along the way, but they do not recognize him. Even as they listen to his teaching they are blind to his presence. But when the bread is broken during the evening meal, their eyes are opened, and they ask themselves:

Did not our hearts burn within us while he talked to us on the road, while he opened to us the scriptures?

Some of us have grown up under the ministry of George Regas to appreciate the breaking of the bread of the eucharist as being at the center of life, not just at the center of the life of the Church, but at the center of the life of the world.

We kneel and weep at the sheer transforming power of this mystery.

We stand in awe of the challenges that God delivers into our hands.

We go forth in the power of the spirit.

www.ingramcontent.com/pod-product-compliance
Lightning Source LLC
Chambersburg PA
CBHW070329230426
43663CB00011B/2265